Blackstone's

Police Q&A

Crime 2005

Blackstone's
Police Q&A

Crime 2005

Third edition

Huw Smart and John Watson

OXFORD
UNIVERSITY PRESS

OXFORD

UNIVERSITY PRESS

Great Clarendon Street, Oxford OX2 6DP

Oxford University Press is a department of the University of Oxford.
It furthers the University's objective of excellence in research, scholarship,
and education by publishing worldwide in

Oxford New York

Auckland Bangkok Buenos Aires Cape Town Chennai
Dar es Salaam Delhi Hong Kong Istanbul Karachi Kolkata
Kuala Lumpur Madrid Melbourne Mexico City Mumbai Nairobi
São Paulo Shanghai Taipei Tokyo Toronto

Oxford is a registered trade mark of Oxford University Press
in the UK and in certain other countries

Published in the United States

by Oxford University Press Inc., New York

A Blackstone Press Book

British Library Cataloguing in Publication Data

Data available

Library of Congress Cataloging in Publication Data

Data available

ISBN 0-19-926833-9

10 9 8 7 6 5 4 3 2 1

Typeset by SNP Best-set Typesetter Ltd., Hong Kong
Printed in Great Britain
on acid-free paper by
Ashford Colour Press Limited, Gosport, Hampshire

Contents

Introduction

Before you get into the detail of this book, there are two myths about multiple choice questions (MCQs) that we need to get out of the way right at the start:

1. that they are easy to answer;
2. that they are easy to write.

Take one look at a professionally designed and properly developed exam paper such as those used by the Police Promotion Examinations Board or the National Board of Medical Examiners in the US and the first myth collapses straight away. Contrary to what some people believe, MCQs are not an easy solution for examiners and not a 'multiple-guess' soft option for examinees.

That is not to say that *all* MCQs are taxing, or even testing — in the psychometric sense. If MCQs are to have any real value at all, they need to be carefully designed and follow some agreed basic rules.

And this leads us to myth number 2.

It is widely assumed by many people and educational organisations that anyone with the knowledge of a subject can write MCQs. You need only look at how few MCQ writing courses are offered by training providers in the UK to see just how far this myth is believed. Similarly, you need only to have a go at a few badly designed MCQs to realise that it is a myth none the less. Writing bad MCQs is easy; writing good ones is no easier than answering them!

As with many things, the design of MCQs benefits considerably from time, training and experience. Many MCQ writers fall easily and often unwittingly into the trap of making their questions too hard, too easy or too obscure, or completely different from the type of question that you will eventually encounter in your own particular exam. Others seem to use the MCQ as a way to catch people out or to show how smart they, the authors, are (or think they are).

There are several purposes for which MCQs are very useful. The first is in producing a reliable, valid and fair test of knowledge and understanding across a wide range of subject matter. Another is an aid to study, preparation and revision for such examinations and tests. The differences in objective mean that there are slight

differences in the rules that the MCQ writers follow. Whereas the design of fully val-
idated MCQs is to be used in high stakes examinations which will effectively determine who passes and who fails have very strict guidelines as to construction, content
and style, less stringent rules apply to MCQs that are being used for teaching and revision. For that reason, there may be types of MCQ that are appropriate in the latter
setting which would not be used in the former. However, in developing the MCQs for
this book, the authors have tried to follow the fundamental rules of MCQ design but
they would not claim to have replicated the level of psychometric rigour that is —
and has to be — adopted by the type of examining bodies referred to above.

These MCQs are designed to reinforce your knowledge and understanding, to
highlight any gaps or weaknesses in that knowledge and understanding and to help
focus your revision of the relevant topics.

I hope that we have achieved that aim.

Good luck!

New to Blackstone's Police Q&As for 2005

References to Blackstone's Police Manuals

For 2005, every answer is followed by a paragraph reference to Blackstone's Police Manuals. This means that once you have attempted a question and looked at an answer, the Manual can immediately be referred to for help and clarification.

Unique numbers for each question

Each question and answer has been given the same unique number. This should ensure that there is no confusion as to which question is linked to which answer. For example, Question 2.1 is linked to Answer 2.1

Checklists

The checklists are designed to help you keep track of your progress when answering the multiple choice questions. If you fill in the checklist after attempting a question, you will be able to check how many you got right on the first attempt and will know immediately which questions need to be revisited a second time.

Acknowledgements

This book has been written as an accompaniment to *Blackstone's Police Manuals*, and will test the knowledge you have accrued through reading that series. It is of the essence that full study of the relevant chapters in each *Police Manual* is completed prior to attempting the Questions and Answers. As qualified police trainers we recognise that students tend to answer questions incorrectly either because they don't read the question properly, or because one of the 'distracters' has done its work. The distracter is one of the three incorrect answers in a multiple choice question (MCQ), and is designed to distract you from the correct answer and in this way discriminate between candidates: the better-prepared candidate not being 'distracted'.

So particular attention should be paid to the *Answers* sections, and students should ask themselves 'Why did I get that question wrong?' and, just as importantly, 'Why did I get that question right?' Combining the information gained in the *Answers* section together with re-reading the chapter in the *Police Manuals* should lead to greater understanding of the subject matter.

The authors wish to thank Katie at Oxford University Press for her support, patience and cajoling skills! Thanks also to Geraldine Mangley at OUP for her invaluable assistance. We would also like to show appreciation to Alistair MacQueen for his vision and support, without which this project would never have been started.

Huw would like to thank both Julie and their beautiful baby Hâf, for their constant strength and support during long evenings and weekends of writing, when he could have been having fun with the family.

John would like to thank Sue for her support; also David, Catherine and Andrew for not too many 'Dad can I have . . .'

1 | State of Mind and Criminal Conduct

STUDY PREPARATION

This chapter, which combines two chapters from the Blackstone's Manuals, tests what could be best described as the general principles of criminal law. When you consider that to prove its case, the prosecution must always prove 'the facts in issue' (*Evidence & Procedure Manual*) beyond a reasonable doubt, then knowledge of the *actus reus* and the *mens rea* becomes very important. In this chapter we will look at the general rule that an offence can be committed only where criminal conduct is accompanied by some element of fault and that both elements must coincide at the same moment in time. The precise fault element required depends upon the particular offence involved, as well as the fact that there is nevertheless a class of offences of 'strict liability', in which no fault element need be proved. In such cases, one can therefore have an *actus reus* without any corresponding *mens rea*. Also tested will be behaviours associated with criminal acts, both by one defendant and also other accessories. When answering questions in this chapter you should remember that although they are based on substantive offences committed, they are testing the general principles of criminal law.

QUESTIONS

Question 1.1

LAWRENCE hates his wife and plans to kill her. He intends to cut her throat on Tuesday morning whilst she is still asleep. On Monday, LAWRENCE picks his wife up from work and is driving home; he is deep in thought about the following day's planned action. Owing to his inattentiveness, LAWRENCE drives through a red light, and his car is struck on his wife's side. She dies as a result of the accident.

Could LAWRENCE be guilty of murder in these circumstances?

A Yes, as he has achieved his desired outcome.

B Yes, as he was thinking about the murder at the time of the accident.

C No, he cannot be guilty of murder in these circumstances.

D No, but he could be guilty of manslaughter.

Question 1.2

In law, some offences require a particular *mens rea*. Burglary, under s. 9(1)(a) of the Theft Act 1968, is such an offence.

What is this type of crime known as? A crime of:

A Specific intent.

B Basic intent.

C Ulterior intent.

D Superior intent.

Question 1.3

In relation to 'negligence', which of the following statements is correct?

A Negligence is concerned with the defendant's standards.

B Negligence is concerned with the defendant's state of mind.

C Negligence is concerned with standards of a reasonable person.

D Negligence is concerned with standards of the law as laid down in statute.

Question 1.4

WHITE was broke and anxious to inherit his mother's money. One night he put potassium cyanide in his mother's bedtime drink with the intention of killing her. In due course, the following morning, it was discovered that his mother had died. WHITE was arrested on suspicion of murder. In fact, WHITE's mother had drunk very little; certainly, nowhere near enough to kill her. She had died of natural causes.

In relation to this, which of the following is true?

A WHITE is guilty of murder as there is a causal link between his actions and his mother's death.

B WHITE is not guilty of any offences as his mother died of natural causes.

C WHITE is guilty of attempted murder due to his intention.

D WHITE is guilty of attempted murder due to his actions, irrespective of his intentions.

Question 1.5

In relation to liability for an offence, which of the following statements is correct?

A A company could be held liable for an offence, but only if the offence is triable summarily.

B An employer cannot be prosecuted for offences committed by his or her employees, as offences are restricted to personal liability.

C A company cannot be prosecuted where an offence requires *mens rea*.

D A company can be prosecuted for an offence which involves strict liability, or where an offence requires *mens rea*.

Question 1.6

JENKINS was in a crowded pub and was larking about with her friends. She decided to throw a pint of beer over her friend BRYANT. Unfortunately the glass slipped out of her hand and smashed in BRYANT's face, causing cuts which required stitches.

In relation to assault occasioning actual bodily harm, what must be proved?

A Intention to commit any type of assault.

B Intention to cause the actually caused.

C Recklessness as to the assault itself.

D Recklessness as to the injury actually caused.

Question 1.7

MATHERS was on his way to hospital to have his appendix removed. JIANIKOS has long had a hatred of MATHERS and sees him just outside the hospital. JIANIKOS punches MATHERS on the head, not that hard. MATHERS, however, has a very weak skull (JIANIKOS had no knowledge of this), and as a result of the blow suffers a serious head injury. The head injury is not life threatening, but the doctors are unable to operate on him. MATHERS' appendix bursts due to this delay in operating, and as a result he dies.

In relation to causation, which of the following is true?

A JIANIKOS has caused the death of MATHERS because of the punch he gave him.

B JIANIKOS has caused the death of MATHERS because there was no intervening act.

C JIANIKOS has not caused the death of MATHERS; there is no link between the punch and the death.

D JIANIKOS has not caused the death of MATHERS, as he had no knowledge of his weak skull.

Question 1.8

ANDREWS was employed to operate a level crossing on a railway whilst a fault with the automated system was repaired. While at work, ANDREWS called his girlfriend on his mobile phone. He was so engrossed in the conversation that he forgot to close the crossing gates when a train was coming. A car was crossing at the time and the train hit it, killing the driver.

Is ANDREWS criminally liable in the death of the driver of the car?

A No, there was no positive action by ANDREWS to cause the accident.

B Yes, he had failed to carry out his duty and is criminally liable.

C No, ANDREWS did not have the relevant *mens rea*.

D Yes, as there is a causal link between his actions and their consequences.

Question 1.9

MILLAR intends to commit a burglary at a local electrical goods shop. He confides in NEWTON, who suggests he does it at 4 a.m. when it will be quieter, and suggests that MILLAR goes through a skylight into a room that is not alarmed. MILLAR thanks him for his advice and goes ahead with the burglary.

What is NEWTON's liability, if any, for the burglary?

A As a counsellor of the offence.

B As a procurer of the offence.

C As a principal offender of the offence.

D He is not liable at all for the offence.

Question 1.10

BALDWIN intends to murder his wife's lover by shooting him. He goes to see BOOKER, whom he knows to be an illegal gun supplier. BALDWIN tells BOOKER what he intends to do, and asks him to supply a gun. BOOKER is unconcerned whether the murder is successful or not, and is only interested in his profit from the deal. BALDWIN commits the murder, but is caught and tells the police about BOOKER.

Is BOOKER an accessory to the murder?

A No, he does not have the required *mens rea*.

B No, as he has no intention of aiding the actual shooting.

C Yes, he is reckless as to whether the shooting will happen or not.

D Yes, he is an accessory to the murder, as he knows the circumstances.

Question 1.11

JONES is a soldier living in the company barracks. JONES has a fight with STEYN during which he stabs him twice in the stomach with a bayonet. Realising the seriousness of STEYN's injuries, two other soldiers carry him to the nearby medical centre. STEYN is a large man and, due to his heavy weight, the soldiers drop him three times on way to the medical centre. On one of those occasions, STEYN hits his head very hard on the ground. On arrival at the centre, the overworked doctor fails to notice that STEYN's lung has collapsed and the treatment he receives from the doctor is less than adequate. STEYN dies from a culmination of all the injuries and the mistreatment he received.

Given the way STEYN was treated after his injury, is JONES criminally liable for STEYN's death?

A Yes, the chain of causation is not broken.
B No, due to the intervening act of the other soldiers.
C No, due to the intervening act of the doctor.
D Yes, provided the stab wound was the major cause of death.

Question 1.12

MURRAY is one of a gang of armed robbers who rob people in their own houses. They plan to go to GRAHAM's house and rob him. MURRAY is aware that knives will be carried, although he will not carry one himself. MURRAY is also aware that the knives may be used for violence, and that the rest of the gang is violent. During the robbery GRAHAM tries to fight back and is stabbed by one of the gang. GRAHAM dies as a result of his injuries.

In order to show that MURRAY is guilty of murder through joint enterprise, what would have to be proved?

A MURRAY agreed to kill, using the knives.
B MURRAY agreed to cause really serious injury using the knives.
C MURRAY agreed to use knives for any purpose.
D MURRAY contemplated that the knife could be used to cause serious bodily injury.

Question 1.13

JONES works for a major retail outlet. Whilst working on the video counter she sells a copy of 'Reservoir Dogs', which holds an '18' classification, to STUART, who is 14 years old.

Given that the boy did not look 18, what is the retail outlet's responsibility with regard to the sale? (This is an offence under s. 11 of the Video Recordings Act 1984.)

A No responsibility, only JONES will have committed the offence.

B No responsibility, unless the manager was aware of the sale.

C Full responsibility under corporate liability.

D Full responsibility under vicarious liability.

Question 1.14

Which of the following best describes, legally, what is meant by recklessness?

A They were aware a risk did exist; in the circumstances known to them they unreasonably took the risk.

B They were aware a risk did or would exist; in the circumstances known to them they unreasonably took the risk.

C They were aware a risk did exist, it was an obvious risk, and they unreasonably took the risk.

D They were aware a risk did or would exist, it was an obvious risk, and they unreasonably took the risk.

ANSWERS

Answer 1.1

Answer **C** — Murder is a crime of specific intent, and requires a specific *mens rea*, i.e. an intention to kill or seriously injure. To be guilty of a criminal offence requiring *mens rea*, an accused must possess that *mens rea* when performing the act or omission in question, and it must relate to that particular act or omission. If, for example, a man accidentally kills his wife in a car crash on Monday, the fact that he was planning to cut her throat on Tuesday does not make him guilty of her murder (which makes answer A wrong), even if he was thinking about the planned murder at the time of the accident (making answer B incorrect), and even if he is subsequently delighted to find that his wife has died. Similarly, he could not be guilty of manslaughter (answer D) which also requires a specific *mens rea*.

Crime, para. 1.1.3.1

Answer 1.2

Answer **C** — Crimes of specific intent are committed only where the defendant is shown to have had a particular intention to bring about a specific consequence at the time of the criminal act. Thus, if burglary, under s. 9(1)(a) of the Theft Act 1968, was breaking a window with intention to enter only, then it would be an offence of specific intent (answer A). Basic intent requires no further proof of anything other than a basic intention to bring about a given circumstance, so if the s. 9(1)(a) offence was simply entering the building as a trespasser then it would be basic intent (answer B). However, as you must show not only intention to enter, but an intention to commit another unlawful act having entered, it is a crime of ulterior intent (answer C). Superior intent has been made up, which makes answer D incorrect.

Crime, paras 1.1.3.1, 1.1.4.1

Answer 1.3

Answer **C** — Some would exclude negligence from a discussion of *mens rea* on the basis that *mens rea* is concerned with states of mind and negligence is not a state of mind (answer B is incorrect) but is rather a failure to comply with the standards of the reasonable person. Unlike strict liability, negligence still ascribes some notion of 'fault' or 'blame' to the defendant who must be shown to have acted in a way that runs contrary to the expectations of the reasonable person. A good example would be that of careless driving: in *Simpson* v *Peat* [1952] 2 QB 24, it was stated that if a driver was 'exercising the degree of care and attention which a reasonable prudent driver would exercise, he ought not to be convicted' of careless driving. It does not matter what the accused actually believes; it is what the reasonable person in the circumstances would have believed which counts (answer A is incorrect). Nor is it the standards laid down by law in statutes (answer D is incorrect).

Crime, para. 1.1.3.3

Answer 1.4

Answer **C** — There are two primary factors to any crime the *mens rea* and the *actus reus*. The mental element, or intention, is vital and there is a presumption that *mens rea* is required for a criminal offence unless parliament clearly indicates otherwise (B (*A minor*) v *DPP* [2000] 2 WLR 452). Therefore, answer D is incorrect. The relevant *mens rea* for attempted murder is intention to kill. WHITE has also taken action by poisoning the drink. However, where *actus reus* is proved, you must show a causal link between that and the relevant consequences. Despite his best efforts she had died, coincidentally, of natural causes. WHITE's conduct had not in any sense contributed to this and he is not guilty of murder (*R* v *White* [1910] 2 KB 124). Therefore, answer A is incorrect. Had he waited just one more day, there would be no criminal liability upon him. However, his intentions together with his actions make him guilty of attempted murder; therefore, answer B is incorrect.

Crime, paras 1.2.2.2, 1.2.4

Answer 1.5

Answer **D** — This question addresses the issues of corporate liability. Companies have been successfully prosecuted for offences involving strict liability (*Alphacell Ltd* v *Woodward* [1972] AC 824) as well as offences which require *mens rea* (*Tesco Supermarkets Ltd* v *Nattrass* [1972] AC 153), making answer C incorrect. Liability is not limited to summary offences (making answer A incorrect), and companies can be liable for the actions of some of their employees under certain circumstances (making answer B incorrect).

Crime, para. 1.2.7

Answer 1.6

Answer **C** — An assault or battery must be committed intentionally or recklessly, so the least you have to prove is recklessness, not necessarily actual intent (making answers A and B incorrect). If injury is caused, it need not even be proved that the injury was foreseeable. This is now clear from the decision of the House of Lords in *R* v *Savage* [1992] 1 AC 699, in which S aimed to throw the contents of a beer glass over B, but inadvertently allowed the glass to slip from her hand and break, with the result that B was injured by it. A conviction for an offence under s. 47 of the Offences Against the Person Act 1861 could be successful, because throwing beer over B was an intentional assault (indeed a battery) and that same assault had resulted in B's injury. Therefore recklessness as to the assault is all that is needed — not recklessness as to the extent of the harm likely to be caused (making answer D incorrect).

Crime, para. 1.1.4.2

Answer 1.7

Answer **A** — Although legal causation must be 'operative and substantial', it need not necessarily be a direct cause of the proscribed result. In *R* v *McKechnie* [1992] Crim LR 194, a man inflicted serious head injuries on another man. These were not in themselves fatal, but they prevented doctors from operating on the injured man's duodenal ulcer, and he died when the ulcer burst. The perpetrator was held to have caused his death. There was a link, therefore answer C is incorrect. In what is known colloquially as the 'Eggshell Skull' rule, a person must ordinarily take his victim as he finds him. If, for example, the victim of an assault is unusually vulnerable to physical injury as a result of an existing medical condition or old age, the person responsible must accept liability for any unusually serious consequences which result. This is true particularly where a blow is struck; answer D is therefore incorrect. In relation to intervening acts, no such intervening act can break the chain of causation if it merely complements or aggravates the ongoing effects of the defendant's initial conduct. The chain of causation can be broken only where the effect of the intervening act is so overwhelming that any initial injuries are completely unconnected to the end result, therefore answer B is incorrect.

Crime, para. 1.2.4

Answer 1.8

Answer **B** — Most offences require a positive act, together with the requisite state of mind for the offence to be complete. However, some offences are brought about by a failure to act, and most of these arise from some sort of duty to act (this makes answers A and C incorrect). A person may in some cases incur criminal liability through failure to discharge his official duties or contractual obligations. A typical example is provided by *R v Pittwood* (1902) 19 TLR 37, in which P was employed to operate a level crossing on a railway but omitted to close the crossing gates when a train was signalled. P was convicted of gross negligence manslaughter. It is not a causal link which requires proof that the consequences would not have happened 'but for' the defendant's actions of omission; here, had the train been even one minute late, the accident would not have happened (answer D is also incorrect).

Crime, para. 1.2.3

Answer 1.9

Answer **A** — A principal offender must meet all the requirements of the particular offence, and for procurement there must be a causal link between his conduct and the offence. Counselling requires no causal link (*R v Calhaem* [1985] QB 808); all that is required is the principal offender's awareness of the counsellor's advice or encouragement — and this is true even if the principal would have committed the offence anyway (*Attorney-General v Able* [1984] QB 795). So he is guilty as a counsellor, not as a principal or procurer (making answers B, C and D incorrect).

Crime, para. 1.2.6

Answer 1.10

Answer **D** — One of the leading cases on the state of mind for accessories is *National Coal Board v Gamble* [1959] 1 QB 11, where Devlin J at p. 20 stated: '. . . aiding and abetting is a crime that requires proof of *mens rea*, that is to say, of intention to aid as well as of knowledge of the circumstances'. However, as Devlin J went on to point out, at p. 23, intention to aid does not require that the accused's purpose or motive must be that the principal offence should be committed:

> If one man deliberately sells to another a gun to be used for murdering a third, he may be indifferent about whether the third man lives or dies and interested only in the cash profit to be made out of the sale, but he can still be an aider and abettor. To hold otherwise would be to negative the rule that *mens rea* is a matter of intent only and does not depend on desire or motive.

There must also be an intention to aid the principal offender, and as such reckless-ness and negligence are not enough to convict an accessory. Thus, answers A, B and C are incorrect.

Crime, para. 1.2.6.1

Answer 1.11

Answer **A** — A defendant will not be regarded as having caused the consequence for which he stands accused if there was a new intervening act sufficient to break the chain of causation between his original action and the consequence in question — in this case the death of STEYN. The chain of causation can be broken only where the effect of the intervening act is so overwhelming that any initial injuries are relegated to the status of mere historical background. In the leading case of *R v Smith* [1959] 2 QB 35, which broadly follows the circumstances outlined in the question, the Courts-Martial Appeals Court held:

> If at the time of death the original wound is still an operating cause and a substantial cause, then the death can properly be said to be the result of the wound, albeit that some other cause of death is also operating. Only if it can be said that the original wounding is merely the setting in which another cause operates can it be said that the death did not result from the wound. Putting it another way, only if the second cause is so overwhelming as to make the original wound merely part of the history can it be said that the death does not flow from the wound.

It follows that a conviction could still be secured. Answers B, C and D are incorrect.

Crime, para. 1.2.5

Answer 1.12

Answer **D** — The main features that will determine MURRAY's liability as an acces-sory in a joint enterprise will be:

- The nature and extent of the agreed offence.
- Whether the accessory knew the principal had a knife.
- Whether a different knife was used.
- Whether the knife was used differently than agreed.

Proof of prior knowledge of the actual crime intended is not necessary if he contem-plated the commission of one of a limited number of crimes by the principal, and in-tentionally assisted in their commission. For an accessory to be found guilty of murder as a joint enterprise it is not necessary for the prosecution to prove that the principal would kill; it is sufficient to prove that he might kill. The accessory, however, will not be guilty where the lethal act carried out by the principal is fundamentally different from the acts foreseen or intended by the accessory: *R* v *Powell* [1999] 1 AC 1.

It is therefore enough that MURRAY contemplated that knives might be used, and that no actual agreement needs to be reached by the parties to the crime; therefore, answers A, B and C are incorrect.

Crime, para. 1.2.6.2

Answer 1.13

Answer **C** — This is an example of an occasion where the knowledge of certain employees will be extended to the company (answer A is incorrect). This was the circumstance in *Tesco Stores Ltd* v *Brent London Borough Council* [1993] 1 WLR 1037, where the Queen's Bench Division held that the knowledge that JONES had about the boy was also knowledge that placed a liability on the corporation. There is no need to prove any positive act by the company (making B incorrect), and it is not vicarious liability as this is mostly committed where a statutory duty has been breached, which is not the case in these circumstances (answer D is incorrect).

Crime, paras 1.2.7, 1.2.8

Answer 1.14

Answer **B** — There have been decades of complex differences between objective and subjective recklessness; thankfully the law has now been clarified. In *R* v *G & R* [2003] 3 WLR 1060, the House of Lords decided that objective recklessness (known as *Caldwell* decisions as set out in *Metropolitan Police Commissioner* v *Caldwell* [1982] AC 341) should be departed from. Their Lordships held that a person acts recklessly (in a criminal damage case):

- With respect to a *circumstance*, when he or she is aware of a risk that exists or would exist.
- With respect to a *result or consequence*, when he or she is aware of a risk that it would occur and it is, in the circumstances known to him or her, unreasonable to take the risk.

This removes the 'it would be obvious to any reasonable bystander' test, therefore answers C and D are incorrect. Also it is more than knowledge that a risk existed; it extends to awareness that a risk would exist — answer A is therefore incorrect.

Crime, para. 1.1.4.2

2 | Incomplete Offences and Police Investigations

STUDY PREPARATION

Having looked at the key building blocks of *mens rea* and *actus reus*, you now need to go on to consider specific criminal offences and their constituent parts. Before doing so, however, you need to get a few problematic situations out of the way.

The first of these deals with those occasions where the defendant, despite his or her best or worst endeavours, fails to do what he or she set out to do. These are 'incomplete' offences. The second area deals with defences to criminal charges — these are addressed in the next chapter.

When dealing with incomplete offences there are two key things to remember: first, that the physical impossibility of actually achieving what the defendant set out to do will not absolve him or her from criminal liability (and why should it?); and secondly, that some offences — such as summary offences and some incomplete offences themselves — cannot be attempted.

Finally, in this chapter we deal with the related area of police operations, where the evidential and substantive issues often overlap with those of the incomplete offences involved.

QUESTIONS

Question 2.1

In which, if any, of the following examples is the common law offence of incitement made out?

1. BROWN, who is 15 years old, encourages her teacher to have unlawful sexual intercourse with her but he does not.
2. FRAMPTON pressurises SMITH to encourage his brother to steal a car for FRAMPTON; however, SMITH's brother does not actually commit the offence.

A Both examples.

B Neither example.

C Example 1 only.

D Example 2 only.

Question 2.2

LANTZOS has been charged with an offence of statutory conspiracy under s. 1 of the Criminal Law Act 1977. He has been charged in respect of an agreement with others to commit a summary offence.

How, if at all, is this case likely to be dealt with?

A Withdrawn because you can only conspire to commit an indictable offence.

B Trial at magistrates' court only.

C Trial at Crown Court only.

D Trial at either magistrates' court or Crown Court.

Question 2.3

JANE and JOHN RICE are married. They plan for JOHN to defraud his insurance company over the reported theft of his car. They involve PEARD in their plan by asking him to hide JOHN's car in his garage until the insurance company pay out. However, a few hours before the plan is initiated, PEARD said he did not want to be involved and the RICEs gave up the idea.

Who, if anyone, is guilty of conspiracy to defraud the insurance company?

A No one as the offence contemplated did not take place.

B No one as you cannot conspire with your spouse.

C JANE and JOHN only.

D All three of them.

Question 2.4

In relation to the offence of conspiracy to defraud, which of the following situations would constitute an offence contrary to common law?

1. WATTS is a collector of model cars, and wishes to make a quick profit. He is aware that GRANT has a rare model Ford Sierra police vehicle, which is white in colour. WATT agrees with GRANT to paint the vehicle red and pass it off at auction as a rarer, more expensive Diplomatic Protection Group police vehicle.
2. TAYLOR is the licensee of the Masons Arms public house, which is wholly owned by a well-known major brewing company. He contacts his friend CROCKET who makes a very potent real ale home brew. They agree to install a barrel of the real ale and sell it at the pub, contrary to the licence TAYLOR holds which allows him to sell only the brewery's beers.

A Situation 1 only.
B Situation 2 only.
C Neither situation.
D Both situations.

Question 2.5

SHARMA has arranged with a burglar to act as a recipient of what he believes to be a stolen video recorder. SHARMA arranges for the video recorder to be delivered to his house on Friday, and it duly arrives. A few hours later the police execute a warrant at his house and find the recorder. Despite extensive enquiries they cannot prove the video recorder was stolen.

Has SHARMA committed the offence of attempting to handle stolen goods?
A No, as he has received the goods he has committed the full offence.
B No, as the goods are not stolen he cannot be guilty of an attempt.
C Yes, he is guilty of attempting to handle the goods when he arranges to receive the goods.
D Yes, he is guilty of attempting to handle the goods when he actually receives the goods.

Question 2.6

In relation to an offence of vehicle interference under s. 9 of the Criminal Attempts Act 1981, which of the following must the prosecution prove to make the offence complete?
A An intention to commit one of the further offences mentioned.
B An intention to commit any of the further offences mentioned.
C An interference only; no intention is needed.
D An interference along with evidence that the vehicle is a motor vehicle.

Question 2.7

YOUNG wishes to kill his wife who will not grant him a divorce, and looks for a contract killer. The police, however, are aware of his plan and send an undercover officer to meet him. YOUNG and the officer agree that for £2,000 the officer, posing as a contract killer, will shoot and kill YOUNG's wife. Naturally the officer has no intention of committing the murder.

In relation to conspiracy, which of the following is true?

A As an agreement has been reached to carry out an offence, this is a statutory conspiracy.

B As an agreement has been reached to carry out an offence, this is a common law conspiracy.

C As the officer will not carry out the murder, the offence of conspiracy is not made out.

D Although the officer will not carry out the murder, YOUNG is still guilty of conspiracy.

Question 2.8

EVANS tries to persuade SCHALK to distribute leaflets in the street. Both persons are aware that the leaflets may stir up racial hatred, and both know it is an offence to distribute these leaflets. EVANS only uses persuasion and does not pressurize or intimidate SCHALK. Although SCHALK took the leaflets, he did not distribute them, he burned them.

In relation to the common law offence of incitement, which of the following is true?

A EVANS has incited SCHALK even although he only used persuasion.

B EVANS has incited SCHALK as SCHALK took the leaflets from EVANS.

C EVANS has not incited SCHALK as no pressure was put on SCHALK.

D EVANS has not incited SCHALK as no offence was committed by SHALK.

Question 2.9

GILLIGAN is very short of cash and decides a robbery of the local post office is his only option. He gets hold of an imitation firearm, which he hides in his coat pocket; he then gets on a bus to the post office. He gets off the bus, and immediately loses his nerve and waits in the queue for another bus to go back home. He is about 10 metres from the entrance to the post office, but never draws his weapon.

2. Incomplete Offences and Police Investigations

At what point, if any, does GILLIGAN commit an offence of attempted robbery?

A When he decides he will commit the robbery.

B When he puts the gun in his pocket.

C When he gets off the bus outside the post office and waits.

D He does not commit an attempted robbery.

Question 2.10

THRUSH is an undercover officer working on a drugs operation. The police are carrying out an operation on GRIMES, a known drug dealer. THRUSH is authorised (proper authorities for this operation have been obtained) to purchase drugs from GRIMES. He approaches GRIMES who offers to sell him a wrap of amphetamine. THRUSH hands over the money and takes the drugs. During the transaction THRUSH asks GRIMES if he can supply a firearm for a robbery he is planning. GRIMES agrees to this and plans a later meeting.

In relation to THRUSH's request, which of the following is true?

A This is not entrapment as GRIMES is volunteering to get the firearms.

B This is not entrapment as the undercover operation has been authorised.

C This may be entrapment as THRUSH is no longer a passive observer.

D This is entrapment as THRUSH was not authorised by the operation to buy firearms.

ANSWERS

Answer 2.1

Answer **B** — Although inciting someone includes pressurising or encouraging some-one to commit an offence, and the other person need not actually commit the substantive offence, there are some exceptions. You cannot incite someone to commit an offence that exists for your own protection (e.g. unlawful sexual intercourse — *R* v *Tyrrell* [1894] 1 QB 710): thus, answers A and C are incorrect. You cannot incite another to aid, abet, counsel or procure an offence which is ultimately not com-mitted (*R* v *Bodin* [1979] Crim LR 176), and therefore answer D is incorrect.

Crime, para. 1.3.2

Answer 2.2

Answer **C** — A charge under this section can be brought for agreements to commit in-dictable or summary offences (answer A is incorrect). However, the offence is only triable on indictment (answers B and D are incorrect).

Crime, para. 1.3.3.1

Answer 2.3

Answer **D** — One of the exclusions to conspiracies is that husband and wife cannot conspire, but this is when they agree together as the sole conspirators. If, however, a husband and wife conspire with a third person who is not a child under 10 or the in-tended victim, all three may be liable to conviction (*R* v *Chrastny* [1991] 1 WLR 1381 confirmed in *R* v *Lovick* [1993] Crim LR 890), and therefore answers B and C are in-correct. Conspiracy does occur even though the offence intended never occurs and therefore answer A is incorrect. Once the agreement is made the offence is complete.

Crime, para. 1.3.3.1

Answer 2.4

Answer **D** — The common law offence of conspiracy to defraud is expressly preserved by s. 5(2) of the Criminal Law Act 1977. It is defined in the leading case of *Scott* v *Metropolitan Police Commissioner* [1975] AC 819, where Viscount Dilhorne said:

... an agreement by two or more [persons] by dishonesty to deprive a person of something which is his or to which he is or would be or might be entitled [or] an agreement by two or more by dishonesty to injure some proprietary right of his suffices to constitute the offence . . .

... it suffices if there is a dishonest agreement to expose the proposed victim to some form of economic risk or disadvantage to which he would not otherwise be exposed.

In the first situation there is clearly an agreement to charge the victim more than he or she should rightly have paid. The second situation deprives the company of its right to sell its own product (see *R* v *Cooke* [1986] AC 909, where buffet car staff were selling their own sandwiches on British Rail trains). Both options are correct and therefore answers A, B and C are incorrect.

Crime, para. 1.3.3.2

Answer 2.5

Answer **C** — This question examines the 'impossibility' rule as it relates to criminal attempts, and the courts have made it clear that an offence can be committed even though it was impossible (*R* v *Shivpuri* [1987] AC 1), as here, where the goods are not stolen (answer B is incorrect). In *Shivpuri*, S was charged with an attempt to commit an offence under s. 3(1) of the Misuse of Drugs Act 1971. He confessed to acting as a recipient and distributor of what he assumed to be an illegally imported drug. It transpired (to his surprise) that the substance was not a drug at all, but he was still guilty of an attempt to commit the s. 3(1) offence. So SHARMA would be guilty when he agrees to receive the goods, an act more than merely preparatory to the substantive offence, i.e. you do not have to wait until he actually receives them (answer D is incorrect). Having received the goods, which are not stolen, he cannot commit a handling offence, as that requires proof that the goods were stolen; therefore, answer A is incorrect.

Crime, para. 1.3.5

Answer 2.6

Answer **B** — This is a crime of specific intent, so you need to prove interference with a motor vehicle or trailer, and as such answer D is incorrect (note there is no definition of what interference is). You do, however, have to show an intention to commit theft of the vehicle/trailer, *or* theft from it *or* TADA (taking and driving away); therefore, C is incorrect. It is not necessary to show intention to commit any particular one of the further offences, and intention to commit any of them would suffice; therefore, answer A is incorrect.

Crime, para. 1.3.4.1

Answer 2.7

Answer **C** — A person cannot be guilty of conspiracy if the only other party to the supposed agreement intends to frustrate or sabotage it. As the officer clearly will frustrate the agreement, answers A and D are incorrect. This was considered by the House of Lords in *Yip Chieu-Chung* v *The Queen* [1995] 1 AC 111, where N, the appellant's only fellow conspirator in a plan to smuggle heroin out of Hong Kong, was an undercover agent working with the knowledge of the authorities. The House of Lords held that if N's purpose had been to prevent the heroin being smuggled, no indictable conspiracy would have existed. Their Lordships said:

> The crime of conspiracy requires an agreement between two or more persons to commit an unlawful act with the intention of carrying it out. It is the intention to carry out the crime that constitutes the necessary *mens rea* for the offence. . . . [A]n undercover agent who has no intention of committing the crime lacks the necessary *mens rea* to be a conspirator.

Conspiracy requires an agreement which will amount to or involve the commission of an offence. Where no such offence is likely, the offence is not made out. Common law conspiracy involves conspiracy to defraud only and therefore B is incorrect.

Crime, para. 1.3.6

Answer 2.8

Answer **A** — A person may incite another to do an act by threatening or by pressure, as well as by persuasion, therefore answer C is incorrect. Incitement can be committed even if the incited person refuses to act, or does not commit the actual offence incited, therefore answer D is incorrect. The offence is complete when the inciter uses persuasion in an attempt to incite another to commit the offence. It is irrelevant that SCHALK took the leaflets; the offence was already committed before this action took place, and answer B is incorrect.

Crime, para. 1.3.2

Answer 2.9

Answer **D** — He does not commit the offence in these circumstances. In *R* v *Gullefer* [1990] 1 WLR 1063, Lord Lane CJ stated that the crucial question was whether the accused had 'embarked upon the crime proper', but that it was not necessary that the accused should have reached a 'point of no return' in respect of the full offence. So at what point in time are the actions of GILLIGAN more than merely preparatory? Certainly his actions involved in getting to the post office were merely preparatory: the forming of the intent (answer A is incorrect); putting the weapon in his pocket (answer B is incorrect). The only time his actions may be more than preparatory is when he is outside the post office. However, intent is the essence of any crime of attempt under the Criminal Attempts Act 1981. The prosecution must ordinarily prove that the accused acted with a specific intent to commit the particular crime attempted. GILLIGAN loses the intent when he steps off the bus, therefore answer C is incorrect. And although he is in proximity to the post office, without the requisite intent he cannot commit attempted robbery.

Crime, para. 1.3.4

Answer 2.10

Answer **C** — The question of police entrapment is an emotive one. Where the line was drawn between legitimate police activity in undercover operations and the police acting as *agents provocateurs* was sometimes fuzzy. The House of Lords laid down the legal position in this issue in *R* v *Loosely; Attorney-General's Reference (No.3) of 2000* [2001] 1 WLR 2060, where it was held, *inter alia*:

> A useful guide is to consider whether the police did no more than present the defendant with an unexceptional opportunity to commit a crime. The yardstick for the purposes of this test is, in general, whether the police conduct preceding the commission of the offence was no more than might have been expected from others in the circumstances.

Was the officer enticing the accused to commit an offence he would not otherwise have committed? He was committing the offence of drug dealing, and was not entrapped there, but the officer goes beyond being a passive observer when he asks about the firearm. In *Loosely*, their Lordships stated:

> The police must act in good faith. Having reasonable grounds for suspicion is one way good faith may be established. It is not normally considered a legitimate use of police power to provide people not suspected of being engaged in any criminal activity with the opportunity to commit crimes. The principle is that the police should prevent and detect crime, not create it.

So the fact the operation was authorised does not negate entrapment by an individual officer (answer A is incorrect); nor does the fact that the accused seems keen to carry out the officer's request (answer B is incorrect). What is also clear is that simply going beyond what is authorised is not necessarily entrapment; it depends on the officer's action — answer D is therefore incorrect. This area of law has guidelines set down, but ultimately it is for the judge to decide if actions amount to entrapment, and whether such entrapment should lead to a stay of proceedings or not. Which is why answer C states 'may be entrapment'.

Crime, para. 1.3.6

There is little point in collecting evidence, arresting and charging a person only to find that they raise a specific or general defence at trial — a defence which the investigating officer could have addressed in interview or when taking witness statements. For this reason alone it is important to know what defences may exist in relation to certain offences. Similarly, as the police are under a duty to investigate fully and impartially, it is important to know what defences may be available to a defendant.

A number of offences have specific defences contained in the relevant statute, and these are (not surprisingly) called statutory defences. In addition, there are a number of 'general defences', some of which are statutory and others existing at common law. It is helpful to divide general defences into two categories:

1. Those which involve a denial of the basic requirements of *mens rea* and voluntary conduct (the defences of mistake and automatism are best regarded in this way).

2. Those which do not deny these basic requirements but which rely on other circumstances of excuse or justification, as in the defences of duress and self-defence.

The integration of the Human Rights Act 1998 and the European Convention on Human Rights into English law is also important in this area of study.

QUESTIONS

Question 3.1

SMITH is driving his motor vehicle at 70 mph in the outside lane of a motorway, with his window open. A bee flies in through the window and, as he fears being stung,

SMITH tries to kill it with his newspaper. Momentarily distracted, he fails to notice the vehicle in front has slowed and he runs into the back of it. Police investigate and he is reported for an offence of careless driving.

In these circumstances could SMITH use the defence of automatism?
A   Yes, his actions were not voluntary or willed.
B   Yes, as he cannot be held liable for his actions as he lost control.
C   No, although a reflex action it would not amount to automatism.
D   Yes, provided he could not have foreseen the bee flying in.

Question 3.2

HERBERT has been arguing over several months with his neighbour, HUGHES, about a shared driveway, and is now at his wits' end. HERBERT decides it is time for action and intends to assault HUGHES to teach him a lesson. Armed with a baseball bat, HERBERT waits for HUGHES to return from work. To aid his courage he drinks half a bottle of scotch, and is intoxicated when HUGHES arrives home. HERBERT runs out and strikes HUGHES over the head with the baseball bat, causing a severe injury. HERBERT has been charged with s. 18 wounding, under the Offences Against the Person Act 1861.

Given that the offence charged is one of 'specific intent', can HERBERT rely on the defence of voluntary intoxication?
A   No, voluntary intoxication can never be a defence.
B   Yes, voluntary intoxication is always a defence for 'specific intent' crimes.
C   Yes, provided he can show he could not form the 'specific intent' whilst intoxicated.
D   No, in these circumstances he could not use this defence.

Question 3.3

THOMPSON has been charged with an offence of murder for killing her husband during a domestic dispute and wishes to claim the defence of insanity. She claims that at the time of committing the offence she was suffering from 'a disease of the mind'.

Who must decide the question of whether THOMPSON was suffering from 'a disease of the mind'?
A   The judge, as it is a question of law.
B   The jury, as it is a question of fact.

C Any doctor, as it is a question of medical opinion.

D A psychologist, as it is a question of specialist medical opinion.

Question 3.4

DUGGAN, a law lecturer, has been stopped by Constable GARDNER to check his driving documents. During the stop, Constable GARDNER believes she can smell alcohol and requests a breath test. DUGGAN takes the test, which is positive, and the officer arrests him. DUGGAN says 'that took longer than 40 seconds to go red, your arrest is unlawful' and tries to leave. The officer stops him and DUGGAN punches her. DUGGAN is charged with an offence of assault with intent to resist arrest. DUGGAN says in interview that he honestly, but mistakenly, believed that the arrest was unlawful.

Considering this offence only, could DUGGAN avail himself of the defence of mistake?

A Yes, provided his belief was genuinely held.

B Yes, as what he did was 'inadvertent'.

C Yes, provided he could show his actions were 'reasonable'.

D No, in these circumstances the defence would not be available.

Question 3.5

NEWMAN, aged 15, has been bullied at school by a gang of youths. The gang are well known for shoplifting in the lunch hour in the local shops. One evening, while his parents were out, NEWMAN received a phone call from one of the gang members, stating that the gang wanted him to steal a pair of trainers from a sports shop on the way into school. The caller stated that if he did not comply, he would be severely beaten the next day in school by members of the gang. NEWMAN was very scared and the next day tried to steal a pair of trainers.

In relation to any possible defence that NEWMAN might have, which of the following is correct?

A NEWMAN would not be able to rely on the defence of duress in these circumstances, as it applies to threats of death only.

B Provided NEWMAN held a genuine belief that he would be seriously injured if he did not commit the crime, he would have a defence of duress in these circumstances.

C NEWMAN would be able to rely on the defence of duress in these circumstances, as a threat was made. It is immaterial whether he believed the threat or not.

D NEWMAN would not be able to rely on the defence of duress in these circumstances, as the threat was not immediate.

Question 3.6

BREWSTER is a member of a gang who, to his knowledge, use loaded firearms to carry out robberies on sub-post offices. The other gang members discuss a forthcoming robbery, and BREWSTER is aware of the plan. During the robbery another member of the gang shoots and kills the sub-post master and they all make good their escape. BREWSTER is later caught and charged with robbery. BREWSTER wishes to use the defence of duress. He claims his wife was threatened at gunpoint after he tried to pull out of the robbery, and he took part only because he feared for his wife's life.

Will BREWSTER be allowed to use duress as a defence?

A   Yes, as his wife's life was threatened.
B   No, the defence will not be available in these circumstances.
C   No, the threat must have been against BREWSTER's life.
D   Yes, provided the person who issued the threat was the one who shot the sub-post master.

Question 3.7

BEVAN parks his car whilst he goes into a restaurant for a meal. He meets a friend and ends up drinking more than he had intended. Believing he would be over the legal limit for driving, BEVAN returns to his car to collect his laptop computer, fully intending to get a taxi. There is now a large gang near his car. The gang are very aggressive and BEVAN fears for his personal safety. As they charge at him, he jumps into his car and drives away. He stops about half a mile further down the road, and parks the car, intending to take a taxi. However, a police officer sees BEVAN and breathalyses him, the result of which is positive. BEVAN is charged with a drink driving offence.

Will BEVAN have a defence to this offence?

A   Yes, he could claim duress.
B   Yes, he could claim duress of circumstances.
C   No, there is no defence to drink driving offences.
D   No, general defences apply to criminal offences only.

Question 3.8

KENDAL has been charged with murder. The circumstances are that whilst engaged in a violent struggle with PEARCE, he struck him with a hammer which caused injuries that led to PEARCE's death. KENDAL is claiming self-defence on the grounds that he had an honestly held belief that the force he used was reasonable in all the circumstances.

If KENDAL's defence succeeds, what will be the outcome at court?

A He will be not guilty of murder, but guilty of manslaughter.

B He will be guilty of murder, but have a greatly reduced sentence.

C He will be not guilty of murder, nor of any other lesser offence.

D He will be not guilty of murder, and will be re-tried for manslaughter.

Question 3.9

Constable EAST is on the tactical firearms unit, and has been called to a hostage situation. Unfortunately, the incident ends when Constable EAST fatally shoots RICHARDS, who was the assailant.

In relation to the lawfulness of EAST's use of lethal force, what test will be applied?

A That he had an honestly held belief that it was necessary.

B That such force was reasonable in the circumstances.

C That such force was no more than absolutely necessary.

D That such force was necessary to protect the life of another.

Question 3.10

HOOD is a keen archer and has permission from THOMAS to use his land for practice. THOMAS even tells him that there is a scarecrow in a field that he can fire at. HOOD takes his high-powered bow and fires an arrow at the scarecrow from 200m. Being a good shot he hits the scarecrow, but is surprised when the scarecrow falls over. He goes to investigate and is horrified to find he has just shot a rambler who had stopped to check his map.

Could HOOD use the defence of mistake if he was charged with murder?

A No, he was under a positive obligation to check what he was aiming at.

B No, he should have checked with the landowner if there was a public footpath.

C Yes, as he had the landowner's authority, the landowner is vicariously liable.

D Yes, as he did not have the requisite *mens rea*.

ANSWERS

Answer 3.1

Answer **C** — The defence of automatism applies only where the loss of control is *total*, which makes answers A and B incorrect. The example in the Manual is where a swarm of bees flew into a car causing the driver to lose control. In the circumstances of the question, a temporary loss of concentration caused by the driver trying to swat the bee could not be seen to be a total loss of control, as is required for the defence to succeed; it is a *voluntary* action by the driver to swat the bee, not a loss of his self-control. This defence does not involve any foresight to certain risks, so answer D is also wrong.

Crime, para. 1.4.2

Answer 3.2

Answer **D** — It is true that voluntary intoxication can sometimes be used as a defence (so answer A is incorrect), even where the crime is one of 'specific intent'. It has been held that where a defendant becomes intoxicated to build up false courage to commit the offence planned, he will not be able to use this defence as he had formed the necessary intent. The intoxication is merely a vehicle to carry out the offence (*Attorney-General for Northern Ireland* v *Gallagher* [1963] AC 349); as he cannot use the defence, answers B and C are incorrect.

Crime, paras 1.4.3, 1.4.3.1

Answer 3.3

Answer **A** — The question of whether a person is suffering from 'a disease of the mind' is a question of law, and therefore the judge must decide and not the jury. Therefore, answer B is incorrect. It is not a question of medical opinion, specialist or not (*R* v *Sullivan* [1984] AC 156), making answers C and D incorrect.

Crime, para. 1.4.4

Answer 3.4

Answer **D** — The defence of mistake will only be used to negate the *mens rea* of the offence charged. The question is 'did the defendant assault the officer to resist arrest'?

The answer is 'yes' and DUGGAN could not claim to have been 'mistaken' as to whether the officer had a power of arrest or not (*R v Lee* [2002], *The Times* 24 October). However, the defence might have been available had he mistakenly believed that the officer was not really a police officer. In the case of *Blackburn v Bowering* [1994] 1 WLR 1324, Sir Thomas Bingham said (at p. 1329): 'the important qualification [is] that the mistake must be one of fact (particularly as to the victim's capacity) and not a mistake of law as to the authority of the person acting in that capacity'. So as answers A, B and C all refer to DUGGAN's belief/actions, they are incorrect as the *mens rea* is clear.

Crime, para. 1.4.5

Answer 3.5

Answer **D** — Generally speaking, where a person is threatened with death or serious physical injury unless he or she carries out a criminal act, he or she may use the defence of duress. Note that this includes a threat of serious injury, not just death, therefore answer A is incorrect (see *R v Graham* [1982] 1 WLR 294). There are, however, caveats to this general use of duress. One of these caveats is that the threatened injury must be anticipated at or near the time of the offence (i.e. not some time in the distant future). As the threat was for the following day NEWMAN could not use the defence, and answers B and C are both incorrect.

Crime, para. 1.4.6

Answer 3.6

Answer **B** — The defence of duress is not available to a person who joins a violent gang, knowing that they might put pressure on him to commit an offence (*R v Sharp* [1987] QB 853). The question follows the broad outline of Sharp. A threat of death or serious harm to a partner may allow the defence of duress (as in *R v Ortiz* (1986) 83 Cr App R 173 where threats to the accused's wife or family were considered to be sufficient). Answers A, C and D all refer to some sort of threat or other, and are made incorrect by the fact that BREWSTER knew that pressure may be applied to him.

Crime, para. 1.4.6

Answer 3.7

Answer **B** — Duress of circumstances is available in traffic cases, so answers C and D are incorrect. BEVAN has to show that his actions were reasonable (*R v Martin* [1989]

1 All ER 652). Here his actions could be regarded as 'reasonable', as he feared for his safety. The fact he stopped soon after supports this claim, and the defence has succeeded in similar circumstances (*DPP* v *Bell* [1992] RTR 335). Contrast this with *DPP* v *Jones* [1990] RTR 33, where a similar defence failed because the accused drove all the way home, without even checking whether he was still being chased. The facts of this question would not support a defence of 'duress' as no threat has been made, which is a necessary component of that defence, which makes answer A incorrect.

Crime, para. 1.4.7

Answer 3.8

Answer **C** — The defence either succeeds, in which case the accused is acquitted, or it fails, in which case the accused will be convicted of murder (so answers A and D are incorrect). Where the defence fails, due to excessive force, there is no scope to argue that self-defence reduces the defendant's liability to manslaughter (*R* v *McInnes* [1971] 1 WLR 1600, confirmed in *R* v *Clegg* [1995] 1 AC 482), so there will be no reduced sentence making answer B incorrect.

Crime, para. 1.4.8.2

Answer 3.9

Answer **C** — The test applied under s. 3(1) of the Criminal Law Act 1967 — such force as is reasonable in the circumstances — has been superseded, as far as lethal force is concerned, by Article 2 of the European Convention on Human Rights. Under the Convention the test for such force is now no more than 'absolutely necessary'; in addition it must be strictly proportionate to the legitimate purpose being pursued. Anything other than this strict test will not be enough, making answers A, B and D incorrect.

Crime, para. 1.4.8

Answer 3.10

Answer **D** — The defences of mistake and inadvertence consist of a denial of the *mens rea* of the particular crime charged. The *mens rea* for murder is the intention to kill or cause grievous bodily harm. So in relation to this defence you can generalise that wherever an offence requires individual awareness of a particular element, a genuine mistake that such an element is absent will be a defence. The logic of this rule is irrefutable as applied to crimes requiring intention. If a man believes he is shooting at an inanimate object such as a scarecrow, he cannot at the same time by that very act intend to kill. Consider the offence of handling stolen goods, where particular information is required. A person who believes that the goods he buys are not stolen cannot at the same time know (or even believe) that the goods are stolen — the two states of mind are logically inconsistent with one another. However, some offences require some degree of foresight or awareness of risk, and these offences create problems for those wishing to avail themselves of this defence; they would have to show ruling out of any risk of the prohibited consequences (see *Chief Constable of Avon and Somerset Constabulary* v *Shimmen* (1986) 84 Cr App R 7). Here the accused claimed to have ruled out the risk of causing damage to a window when he aimed a martial-art-style kick in its direction, basing his view on his faith in his own prowess as an exponent of the Korean art of self-defence. In other words, he claimed to believe that no damage would result from his action (the subsequent shattering of the window revealing this belief to be a sadly mistaken one). So HOOD, if charged with murder, would not have to show foresight of what he was aiming at, or whether there might be a person as opposed to an inanimate object in the field, where he was to use this defence; answers A and B are therefore incorrect. And even with the landowner's permission, were HOOD to have the requisite *mens rea* for murder, this defence would not be available; answer C is therefore incorrect.

Crime, para. 1.4.5

4 | Homicide

STUDY PREPARATION

This short chapter contains the law relating to some of the most serious charges a person can face. Although these offences are still relatively rare and are usually dealt with by specialist investigators, it is important to know the constituent elements — particularly as it is often more a case of good fortune which prevents people involved in assaults and woundings from facing these more serious charges. In addition to the offences themselves, the chapter deals extensively with the special defences associated with an indictment for murder. It is worth noting that there are three different types of manslaughter offences, and it is worth learning the differences between them.

QUESTIONS

Question 4.1

WILSON has had a stormy relationship with his girlfriend, who is now seven months' pregnant. One night in a fit of rage he hits her so hard she falls and bangs her head on the wall. She is taken into hospital and goes into early labour. The child is born alive but dies three days later. When interviewed by police, WILSON admits that his intention was only to cause serious injury to the mother.

Which is the most appropriate charge relating to the death of the baby?

- **A** Murder.
- **B** Manslaughter.
- **C** Grievous bodily harm owing to transferred malice of intention.
- **D** No offence in relation to the death of the baby.

Question 4.2

There are three special defences open to a person charged with an offence of murder. Should they be successful, what is the legal effect of these defences?

A They would allow an acquittal.

B They would allow a conviction of manslaughter.

C They would allow a partly reduced sentence.

D They would allow a greatly reduced sentence.

Question 4.3

HUSSLEBEE is infuriated that her husband has been having an affair for the last three years and confronted her husband and his lover, MARTIN, whilst they were out on a date. HUSSLEBEE is furious and close to losing restraint; her husband says 'she is far better in bed than you and gives great blow jobs'. MARTIN laughs loudly and points at HUSSLEBEE. Completely losing self-control HUSSLEBEE picks up a wine bottle and hits MARTIN over the head with it. MARTIN subsequently dies from her injuries. HUSSLEBEE is charged with murder.

Considering the defence of provocation for HUSSLEBEE, which of the following is true?

A She cannot claim 'provocation', as MARTIN did not use words to provoke her.

B She cannot claim 'provocation', as she did not attack the person who provoked her.

C She can claim 'provocation', even though she attacked MARTIN for only laughing.

D She can claim 'provocation by circumstances' due to the circumstances of the affair.

Question 4.4

AMIR, BROOKES and SHARP decide they want to end their lives and form a written agreement. They intend to shoot each other in a game of Russian roulette which involves loading a gun with four bullets, one of which is a blank. They load the revolver and spin the chamber. AMIR fatally shoots BROOKES in the head, and then SHARP fatally shoots AMIR in the head. SHARP then turns the gun on himself but the next bullet is blank. Thankful to be alive, SHARP panics and runs from the scene.

In relation to suicide pacts, if SHARP is to use this as a 'special defence' to murder, which of the following must be shown?

A Only that such a pact existed at the time SHARP shot AMIR.
B That a pact existed and that SHARP intended to shoot himself next.
C That a written agreement existed between AMIR and SHARP.
D That a written agreement existed between all the parties.

Question 4.5

ARMSTRONG is a well-known drugs dealer. He supplies BROWN with a wrap of heroin, which ARMSTRONG knows is dangerous due to its purity. BROWN goes home and injects the heroin into his vein. The heroin is so pure it kills him.

In relation to ARMSTRONG's conduct, which of the following statements is true?
A It amounts to manslaughter by unlawful act.
B It amounts to manslaughter by gross negligence.
C It does not amount to any offence of homicide.
D It amounts to murder.

Question 4.6

NEAL and MENDEZ were hunting fanatics. While hunting in the local woods, NEAL thought he would play a joke on MENDEZ. NEAL pointed his rifle at MENDEZ, be-lieving there were no bullets in the chamber, and pulled the trigger. However, he had not checked the gun properly and MENDEZ was hit by a bullet in the chest. MENDEZ was taken to the local hospital, where he subsequently died.

In relation to any homicide offences committed by NEAL, which of the following is correct?
A NEAL is guilty of murder in these circumstances, as he was reckless in his actions.
B NEAL is guilty of manslaughter in these circumstances, as he was reckless in his actions.
C NEAL is not guilty of manslaughter by an unlawful act, as he had no intention to injure MENDEZ.
D NEAL is guilty of manslaughter in these circumstances, as he was negligent in relation to his gun.

Question 4.7

BRANDRICK has been charged with an offence of attempted murder. What is the *mens rea* required to support such a charge?
A Intention to kill the victim.

B Intention to cause grievous bodily harm.

C Intention either to kill the victim or to cause grievous bodily harm.

D Recklessness as to whether the victim dies or not.

Question 4.8

DEEN is an ardent and devout Muslim who created audiotapes for others to listen to. These were of an inflammatory nature and urged Muslims to fight and kill, among others, Jews, Christians, Americans, Hindus and other unbelievers. He encouraged his listeners to kill. He encouraged them to wage Jihad against the enemies of Islam as he deemed them to be. When questioned by police, DEEN stated that when he spoke of killing, he was speaking only of killing in self-defence.

Is this solicitation to murder?

A No, as he did not personally encourage, only through the tapes.

B No, as there was no specific threat against someone.

C No, as he has not coerced people to murder for him.

D Yes, as he has sought to solicit and encourage murder.

ANSWERS

Answer 4.1

Answer **B** — The House of Lords decided in *Attorney-General's Reference (No. 3 of 1994)* [1998] AC 245 that the unborn child is not simply a part of its mother but that they are distinct organisms. They also held, however, that the doctrine of transferred malice does not fully apply, and therefore answer C is incorrect. An intention to inflict grievous bodily harm on the mother cannot attract liability for murder in respect of the subsequent death of the child (answer A is incorrect), although there will still be a liability for the death of the child, answer D is therefore incorrect. If the intention was to kill the mother and to cause the child to die after having been born alive, there may be an offence of murder but we are not told this in the facts given.

Crime, para. 1.5.2

Answer 4.2

Answer **B** — There are three special defences to murder and all three are governed by the Homicide Act 1957. All three are partial defences, reducing the offence from murder to manslaughter rather than leading to an outright acquittal. Answer A is therefore incorrect. These defences are needed principally because the mandatory life sentence for murder does not leave any discretion to the judge in sentencing whereby he or she can take account of factors such as provocation, as would normally be the case with lesser offences where the sentence is not fixed by law. Consequently, answers C and D are incorrect.

Crime, para. 1.5.3

Answer 4.3

Answer **C** — Note that this question asks you if she can claim the defence of provocation, not whether it will succeed or not. You are not asked to judge that 'a reasonable person' would have acted as HUSSLEBEE did. What is important is that she had a sudden loss of control (the question tells you that) and that there was 'provocation'.

First, provocation is no longer restricted to 'some act, or series of acts', since s. 3 of the Homicide Act 1957, by its use of the phrase 'whether by things done or by things said or by both together', clearly visualises that words alone can constitute provocation (see *DPP* v *Camplin* [1978] AC 705 *per* Lord Diplock at p. 716). The acts, words, or indeed sounds, may even be perfectly lawful or commonplace ones as, for example, the crying of a young baby (*R* v *Doughty* (1986) 83 Cr App R 319); therefore, answer A is incorrect.

Secondly, it appears it no longer need be 'something done by the dead man to the accused'. It may be something done by a third person in some way connected with the victim (see *R* v *Davies* [1975] QB 691, conduct by wife's lover relevant to whether husband provoked to kill his wife); therefore, answer B is incorrect. Provocation, however, does seem to require conduct on the part of someone, and there is no such thing as provocation by circumstances (*R* v *Acott* [1997] 1 WLR 306). Therefore, answer D is incorrect.

Crime, para. 1.5.3.2

Answer 4.4

Answer **B** — A suicide pact is formed when a common agreement is made between two or more persons, having for its object the death of all of them. It does not have to be written, but does have to be an agreement between all involved. A suicide pact allows for a conviction of manslaughter, and not murder, where the accused was acting in pursuance of such a pact.

The defendant must show that a suicide pact had been made, *and* he or she had the intention of dying at the time the killing took place. (Therefore, answers C and D are incorrect.)

This means that the existence of the pact is not enough (answer A is therefore incorrect) — at the time of the killing there must also be an intention of dying.

Crime, para. 1.5.3.3

Answer 4.5

Answer **C** — As a starting point you should ask, 'Was the dealer's intention to kill or cause grievous bodily harm to the user?'. If not, the offence of murder will not be made out and therefore answer D is incorrect. Manslaughter by gross negligence requires a degree of negligence by the accused. Here Armstrong was not negligent in supplying the drugs, nor when Brown injected himself (therefore answer B is incorrect). The actions of the user (the self injection) breaks the chain of causation between the unlawful supply and the cause of the death, and therefore the dealer is not responsible for the death of the user (*R* v *Dalby* [1982] 1 WLR 62 and *R* v *Armstrong* [1989] Crim LR 149) — answer A is incorrect.

Crime, para. 1.5.4.1

Answer 4.6

Answer **C** — Like most offences, homicide requires that the defendant had the required *mens rea* for the relevant 'unlawful act', which for homicide offences would lead to the death of a victim. If the defendant did not have that *mens rea*, the offence of manslaughter will not be made out and therefore answers A, B and D are incorrect. In the case of *R* v *Lamb* [1967] 2 QB 981, the defendant pretended to fire a revolver at his friend. Although the defendant believed that the weapon would not fire, the chamber containing a bullet moved round to the firing pin and the defendant's friend was killed. As Lamb did not have the *mens rea* required for an assault his conviction for manslaughter was quashed.

Crime, para. 1.5.4.1

Answer 4.7

Answer **A** — According to CPS Charging Standards, para 10.3, 'unlike murder, which requires an intention to kill or cause grievous bodily harm, attempted murder requires evidence of an intention to kill alone'. Thus an intention to kill is the required *mens rea* for this offence and therefore answers B, C and D are incorrect.

Crime, para. 1.5.2; CPS Charging Standards, Appendix 1.2

Answer 4.8

Answer **D** — There is no requirement that the solicitation be made in person (answer A is incorrect), nor that there be a particular person under threat (answer B is incorrect). The scope of the behaviour sufficient to constitute the offence was classically identified as follows in *R* v *Most* (1881) 7 QBD 244 *per* Huddleston B, at p. 258:

> The largest words possible have been used — 'solicit' — that is defined to be, to importune, to entreat, to implore, to ask, to attempt to try to obtain: 'encourage', which is to intimate, to incite to anything, to give courage to, to inspirit, to embolden, to raise confidence, to make confident, 'persuade' which is to bring any particular opinion, to influence by argument or expostulation, to inculcate by argument: 'endeavour' and then, as if there might be some class of cases that would not come within those words, the remarkable words are

used, 'or shall propose to', that is say, make merely a bare proposition, an offer for consideration.

This wide interpretation means that coercion is not required; therefore answer C is incorrect. The facts of this question mirror that of *R* v *El-Faisal* [2004] EWCA Crim 343, where the Court of Appeal upheld the conviction of El-Faisal for solicitation to murder through the production of tapes that urged Muslims to kill unbelievers.

Crime, para. 1.5.6

5 | Misuse of Drugs

STUDY PREPARATION

Offences relating to the misuse of drugs require a sound knowledge both of the elements of the offences and the case law that supports them. You should also understand the elements of the statutory defences that apply, and how they affect the case in question. This chapter also covers the rather complicated power to enter, search and seize granted by s. 23 of the Misuse of Drugs Act 1971, and it is well worth taking your time over this section (if you've read it you'll know what I mean!). In addition to the more usual controlled drugs, this chapter also includes the law relating to intoxicating substances.

QUESTIONS

Question 5.1

Constable FOSTER asks your advice regarding the offence of supplying articles for administration or preparing controlled drugs (under s. 9A of the Misuse of Drugs Act 1971). She has received information regarding HAINING, who is supplying hypodermic syringes to drug users who are using them to inject themselves with heroin. Constable FOSTER asks you what action she can take.

In relation to the above offence, which of the following is correct?

A   Constable FOSTER can apply for a search warrant under the 1971 Act.

B   Constable FOSTER can arrest HAINING for committing the offence.

C   Constable FOSTER can report HAINING for committing the offence.

D   The offence is not complete; hypodermic syringes are not included in this offence.

Question 5.2

GOSS has a bottle of vitamin tablets in her handbag. Unknown to her, her son had put three Ecstasy tablets in the bottle that morning. Before leaving the house GOSS checks that she has the bottle in her handbag.

Which of the following is correct?

A GOSS is in possession of a controlled drug, but may not be committing an offence.

B GOSS is in possession of a controlled drug and is committing an offence.

C GOSS is not in possession of a controlled drug as she did not put them in the bottle.

D GOSS is not in possession of a controlled drug as she has no knowledge of what they are.

Question 5.3

Detective Constable JONES is a member of the National Crime Squad. She has been involved in an undercover operation in relation to drug trafficking. STEER is a major drug dealer and has asked JONES to help in the supply of cocaine. JONES has provisionally agreed to this to maintain her cover. In fact JONES has no intention of illegally supplying drugs, and an arrest of STEER is imminent.

In relation to incitement under s. 19 of the Misuse of Drugs Act 1971, which of the following is correct?

A The offence is complete when STEER asks JONES to supply the drugs.

B As JONES has no intention of supplying the drugs, the offence is not complete.

C The offence would be complete only if JONES actually supplied the drugs.

D The offence is complete only if STEER receives the drugs, and supplying is complete.

Question 5.4

PATEL is a self-employed chemist and her partner, NEWMAN, confessed to her that he was a heroin addict, although not registered as such. PATEL was shocked by the news, but agreed to help NEWMAN break his addiction. PATEL took some methadone from her storeroom, and gave it to NEWMAN.

In relation to PATEL's actions, which of the following is incorrect?

A PATEL has committed no offence in these circumstances, as she had lawful possession of the drug.

B Even though PATEL would normally be entitled to lawfully possess a controlled drug, she has committed an offence by supplying it to NEWMAN.

C PATEL has committed an offence in these circumstances.

D PATEL has committed an offence from the time she took the drug from the surgery intending to supply it to NEWMAN.

Question 5.5

Consider the following situations. In which, if either, will MEREDITH be able to claim a statutory defence to the offence of possession of a controlled drug?

1. She finds white powder, which she believes is cocaine, in her son's room. She takes it, intending to flush it down the toilet. However, as a leader of the local youth club, she decides to keep it to show her co-leaders so they will be able to recognise the drug should they find any.

2. She finds a quantity of ecstasy tablets, which she buries in the back garden, hoping nature will take its course and destroy the drugs.

A Situation 1 only.

B Situation 2 only.

C Both situations.

D Neither situation.

Question 5.6

HAMMOND is a customs officer working undercover. She is part of an on-going operation regarding drug supply at the 'Green Man' public house. The officer goes to the pub to make a test purchase, and is shown several wraps containing white powder by HAYES, a suspected drug dealer. HAYES states that the wraps contain amphetamine and will cost £30 per wrap. In fact the wraps contain baking powder, a fact of which HAYES is unaware. The transaction takes place.

Which of the following offences, if any, does HAYES commit?

A Possession of a controlled drug.

B Possession with intent to supply a controlled drug.

C Offering to supply a controlled drug.

D Supplying a controlled drug.

Question 5.7

BARTON and HOLLOWAY are business partners. HOLLOWAY uses her factory for the production of Ecstasy. BARTON ensures that the premises are not disturbed by providing 24-hour security in the factory, and also provides transportation to the factory of the raw goods required for the production of Ecstasy. BARTON neither visits the factory, nor has any direct contact with the security or transportation, but is aware of what happens at the factory. HOLLOWAY never visits the factory either.

Who, if anyone, is guilty of unlawful production of a controlled drug under s. 4 of the Misuse of Drugs Act 1971?

A BARTON.

B HOLLOWAY.

C Both of them.

D Neither of them.

Question 5.8

BOOKER has long been suspected by the police of being involved in the supply of controlled drugs and a warrant has been obtained to search his premises. The police go to BOOKER's house and, as they enter, BOOKER takes various papers and shreds them. BOOKER is unsure whether they are evidence or not, but is not willing to take a chance. These papers actually amounted to the only real evidence proving BOOKER's involvement in the supply of controlled drugs.

Has BOOKER committed an offence of obstruction under s. 23(4) of the Misuse of Drugs Act 1971?

A Yes, he was reckless as to whether the papers were evidence or not.

B Yes, he has obstructed the officers by destroying the evidence.

C No, as obstruction only applies to deliberate, physical obstruction of the officers themselves.

D No, as obstruction only applies to stop/searches in relation to drugs.

Question 5.9

Police officers involved in intelligence operations may have to commit acts that are unlawful by virtue of the Misuse of Drugs Act 1971. The officers, as well as other professionals, are exempted from the 1971 Act by the Misuse of Drugs Regulations 2001.

In relation to these exemptions, which, if either, of the following statements is/are correct?

1. Police officers may keep controlled drugs in their possession.

2. Police officers may supply controlled drugs to another.

A Statement 1 only.

B Statement 2 only.

C Both statements.

D Neither statement.

Question 5.10

GORDON has a controlled drug in his pocket, which he intends to supply to someone else. Seeing a police officer in the distance, he hands the drugs to his friend, MERED-ITH, and says 'hold on to these for me and I will give you £20'. MEREDITH agrees and takes possession of the drugs. The officer walks past them and MEREDITH hands the drugs back to GORDON and collects his £20.

In relation to the controlled drugs, which offence(s) has MEREDITH committed?

A Possession only.

B Supply only.

C Possession or supplying only.

D Possession or supplying or possession with intent to supply.

Question 5.11

GOULD is 16 years old and works on Saturdays in his father's shop. He sells a bottle of solvent to his school friend whom he knows is 16 years old.

Under s. 1 of the Intoxicating Substances (Supply) Act 1985 (supply of an intoxicating substance), which of the following is correct in relation to the defences available to GOULD?

A GOULD has a defence owing to his age only.

B GOULD has a defence as he was acting in the course of a business.

C GOULD has a defence owing to his age and the fact that he was acting in the course of a business.

D GOULD has no defence.

Question 5.12

LAING was in possession of cocaine, which he firmly believed to be amphetamine. He is supplying the drug, and has clingfilm, scales and paper on him to assist in this supply.

Considering the offence of possession with intent to supply (s. 5(3), Misuse of Drugs Act 1971), which of the following is correct?

A The prosecution must prove that it was a controlled drug and that he knew it was a controlled drug.

B The prosecution must prove that is was cocaine, and that LAING suspected that is was cocaine.

C The paraphernalia in his possession is evidence of his intention to supply.

D It is immaterial that he thought it was some other type of drug; possession with intent is enough.

Question 5.13

A travel restriction order made under the Criminal Justice and Police Act 2001 to restrict the travel of convicted drug traffickers lasts for a maximum of what period?

A Two years.

B Four years.

C Ten years.

D Unlimited period; no set maximum.

Question 5.14

MAY was the sole tenant and occupier of a flat, which was raided by the police. They found MAY, along with seven others, and a number of items used for the smoking of drugs. They also found a quantity of cannabis resin. MAY admits he had given permission for drug smoking to take place. During the search of the premises the police could detect no smell of cannabis. MAY was charged with allowing the offence of permitting the smoking of cannabis, cannabis resin or prepared opium on premises under s. 8 of the Misuse of Drugs Act 1971.

Is MAY guilty of this offence?

A Not guilty, as he was not the owner of the premises.

B Not guilty, as there was no evidence actual smoking took place.

C Guilty, as there was cannabis and drugs paraphernalia in the premises.

D Guilty, as he admits that he gave permission for drug smoking.

Question 5.15

Police are considering a closure notice under s. 1 of the Anti-social Behaviour Act 2003, with regard to a club which has been used in connection with supplying Class A drugs.

In relation to the officer who can authorise this, and how long this individual can go back in relation to the club's activities (the officer is considering issuing the order today), which of the following is true?

A An assistant chief constable (ACC) can authorise, and can consider the use of the club over the past month.

B A Superintendent can authorise, and can consider the use of the club over the past month.

C An ACC can authorise, and can consider the use of the club over the past three months.

D A Superintendent can authorise, and can consider the use of the club over the past three months.

Question 5.16

Police officers are executing a warrant under s. 23 of the Misuse of Drugs Act 1971 at a house. The warrant allows for the searching of persons as well as the premises. In the house are several people, including a gas meter reader, who states he was there to read the meter. The police wish to search him, but he wants to go and read other meters.

Which of the following is true?

A They can search the meter reader, but only with his permission.

B They can search the meter reader, and can require him to remain for that purpose.

C They cannot search the meter reader, only the occupier of the premises.

D They cannot search him, only the occupier and persons present with his permission.

Question 5.17

Section 4 of the Anti-social Behaviour Act 2003 creates offences of remaining in or entering property without reasonable excuse, subject to a closure notice or order, and of obstructing a constable or authorised person carrying out certain functions under the provisions of the 2003 Act.

What is the power given to police to deal with offenders?

A A constable in uniform may arrest in these circumstances.

B A constable may arrest using the statutory power of arrest.

C A constable may arrest, as they are arrestable offences.

D Report offenders for summons; there is no specific power of arrest.

ANSWERS

Answer 5.1

Answer **D** — This offence deals with the supplying of or offering to supply articles for use for preparing or administering controlled drugs. The offence is designed to address the provision of drug 'kits'. It specifically does not include hypodermic syringes, or parts of them (s. 9A(2)). The administration for which the articles are intended must be 'unlawful'. As the offence has not been committed, there is no action that the officer can take to either search or bring HAINING before justice, and therefore answers A, B and C are incorrect. The offence has no specific power of arrest.

Crime, para. 1.6.8.8

Answer 5.2

Answer **A** — Common law outlines possession as physical control plus knowledge of the presence of the drugs. This becomes problematical where the person in possession claims not to realise what they possessed. In these cases you need to show that the person had physical control of the container together with knowledge that it contained something. GOSS knew she had a container and that it contained tablets (answers C and D are therefore incorrect). This simply means that GOSS was in possession of controlled drugs, not that she was committing an offence under the 1971 Act. It is clear from various case authorities that the basic elements are that a person 'knows' that they are in possession of something which is in fact a controlled substance. As answer C states that she is committing an offence for simply possessing the drugs, it is incorrect. She may commit an offence, as outlined in answer A; however, she could avail herself of the statutory defences available.

Crime, para. 1.6.5

Answer 5.3

Answer **A** — The definition of this offence under s. 19 of the Misuse of Drugs Act 1971 is 'for a person to incite . . . another to commit [an offence under this Act]'. This clearly covers all sections, not just supplying.

Although the offence of incitement exists for most other offences generally, the 1971 Act makes a specific offence of inciting another to commit an offence under its provisions.

On the arguments in *DPP* v *Armstrong* [2000] Crim LR 379, it would seem that a person inciting an undercover police officer may commit an offence under this section even though there was no possibility of the officer actually being induced to commit the offence, and therefore answer B is incorrect. As the offence is committed at the time the incitement is made and is not conditional on either the supply or receipt of the controlled drugs, answers C and D are incorrect.

Crime, para. 1.6.8.18

Answer 5.4

Answer **A** — Section 5 of the Misuse of Drugs Act 1971 states:

(3) Subject to section 28 of this Act, it is an offence for a person to have a controlled drug in his possession, whether lawfully or not, with intent to supply it to another in contravention of section 4(1) of this Act.

It is important to note that the lawfulness or otherwise of the possession is irrelevant; what matters here is the lawfulness of the intended supply. If a vet, or a police officer or some other person is in lawful possession of a controlled drug but they intend to supply it unlawfully to another, this offence will be made out.

This is a crime of specific intent and the intention to supply would have to be proven, as it is in the question. Consequently, PATEL commits an offence, making answers B, C and D actually correct in law. The question, though, asks you what is incorrect, and therefore answer A is actually the correct answer.

Crime, para. 1.6.8.6

Answer 5.5

Answer **D** — Defences are provided by s. 5 of the Misuse of Drugs Act 1971, which states:

(4) In any proceedings for an offence under subsection (2) above in which it is proved that the accused had a controlled drug in his possession, it shall be a defence for him to prove —
   (a) that, knowing or suspecting it to be a controlled drug he took possession of it for the purpose of preventing another from committing or continuing to commit an offence in connection with that drug and that as soon as possible after taking possession of it he took all such steps as were reasonably open to him to destroy the drug or to deliver it into the custody of a person lawfully entitled to take custody of it; or

(b) that, knowing or suspecting it to be a controlled drug he took possession of it for the purpose of delivering it into the custody of a person lawfully entitled to take custody of it and that as soon as possible after taking possession of it he took all such steps as were reasonably open to him to deliver it into the custody of such a person.

In the first situation, having taken initial steps to destroy the drug, MEREDITH could claim a defence under subsection (4)(a). However, when she then decides to keep the cocaine she loses that right and would be in unlawful possession. Consequently, as situation 1 does not give rise to a defence, answers A and C are incorrect. In the second situation, which is a fairly technical issue in relation to the defence, the Administrative Court supported the view that relying on the forces of nature did not provide this defence (*R v Murphy* [2003] 1 WLR 422). At the original trial of the accused for burying cannabis the trial judge had not left it open to the jury to consider the defence, and even on appeal this approach was endorsed. Consequently, situation 2 does not give rise to a defence and answer B is also incorrect.

Crime, para. 1.6.7

Answer 5.6

Answer **C** — For the offences of possession, possession with intent to supply and supply, the prosecution would need to prove that the substance in question is in fact a controlled drug. Answers A, B and D are therefore incorrect. For the offence of offering to supply under s. 4(c) of the 1971 Act, it does not matter whether the accused had a controlled drug in his or her possession or had easy access to a controlled drug.

Crime, para. 1.6.8.2

Answer 5.7

Answer **C** — The meaning of 'produce' and 'concerned in production' is defined by s. 37 of the Misuse of Drugs Act 1971, which states:

(1) ... 'produce', where the reference is to producing a controlled drug, means producing it by manufacture, cultivation or any other method, and 'production' has a corresponding meaning; ...

Being concerned in production requires the accused to take an identifiable role in the production. Both BARTON and HOLLOWAY take an identifiable role in the production in that, although they never visit the premises, they have guilty knowledge of its function and, but for their actions, the production may not take place. This makes option C the only possible correct answer.

Crime, para. 1.6.8.1

Answer 5.8

Answer **B** — This offence is complete where the person obstructs someone carrying out stop/search procedures and also executing a warrant, and therefore answer D is incorrect. In *R v Forde* (1985) 81 Cr App R 19, it was held that a person only committed this offence if the obstruction was intentional, that is to say the act viewed objectively, through the eyes of a bystander, did obstruct the constable's search, and viewed subjectively, that is to say through the eyes of the accused himself, was intended so to obstruct. BOOKER knew he was intentionally obstructing the officers and, even though he was unsure of the outcome, recklessness does not apply (answer A is incorrect). Section 23(4)(b) of the Misuse of Drugs Act 1971 states that the offence includes a person who 'conceals from a person acting in the exercise of his powers under subsection (1) above any such books, documents . . .'. So, as books and documents are included, answer C is incorrect.

Crime, para. 1.6.9.2

Answer 5.9

Answer **C** — Regulation 6 of the Misuse of Drugs Regulations 2001 provides that certain people, including police officers in the course of their duty, may possess and supply controlled drugs to others under very strict conditions. Both these statements are correct and as such answers A, B and D are incorrect.

Crime, para. 1.6.6

Answer 5.10

Answer **D** — In its simplest form, where one person hands over a controlled drug to another, there can be said to be a supply. Where a person leaves a controlled drug with another for safekeeping, the situation is trickier. Fortunately, the House of Lords have given direction in this area in two cases: *R v Maginnis* [1987] AC 303 and *R v Dempsey and Dempsey* (1986) 82 Cr App R 291. The outcome of these cases is that if the person looking after the drugs for another is in some way benefiting from that activity, then the return of those drugs to the depositor will amount to 'supplying' and the offences supplying or possession with intent to supply will be applicable as well as simple possession. None of these offences need stand alone in the circumstances outlined in the question, and therefore answers A, B and C are incorrect.

Crime, para. 1.6.8

Answer 5.11

Answer **D** — Section 1 of the Intoxicating Substances (Supply) Act 1985 defines the defence in subsection (2) as:

> in proceedings against any person for an offence under subsection (1) above it is a defence for him to show that at the time he made the supply or offer he was under the age of 18 and was acting otherwise than in the course or furtherance of a business.

So on the one hand GOULD does have a defence in that he is 16; but this does not stand alone as the statute says 'under the age of 18 *and'* — that 'and' makes answer A incorrect. The second part of the subsection concerns 'acting otherwise than in the course or furtherance of a business' and as GOULD was acting in the course of or in furtherance of a business, he is not afforded this defence and answers B and C are incorrect.

Crime, para. 1.6.10

Answer 5.12

Answer **D** — The prosecution only has to establish that the accused was in possession of the controlled drug as charged with the necessary intent. The accused will not be able to avail himself of the defences in s. 28(2) or 28(3)(b)(ii) where he believed the substance to be a different drug from that alleged by the prosecution, as it is not necessary for the prosecution to prove which controlled drug it was in order to obtain a conviction (*R v Leeson* [2000] 1 Cr App Rep 233); therefore, answers A and B are incorrect. Although possession of drugs paraphernalia will be relevant evidence to show a tendency to be involved in drugs dealing, it does not prove the intention to supply, and careful direction by the judge is needed in outlining its probative value (*R v Haye* [2003] Crim LR 287); therefore, answer C is incorrect.

Crime, para. 1.6.8.6

Answer 5.13

Answer **D** — The introduction of the Criminal Justice and Police Act 2001, ss. 33–37, allows any criminal court (but effectively, given the sentencing restriction, this means the Crown Court) to impose a travel restriction order on an offender who is convicted of a drug trafficking offence. The offender has to have been sentenced by that court to a term of imprisonment for four years or more (s. 33(1)). The effect of the order is to restrict the offender's freedom to leave the United Kingdom for a period specified by the court, and it may require delivery up of his passport. The minimum duration of a travel restriction order is two years, starting from the date of the offender's release from custody. There is no maximum period prescribed in the legislation, therefore answers A, B and C are incorrect. The court must always consider whether such an order should be made and must give reasons where it does not consider such an order to be appropriate (s. 33(2)).

Crime, para. 1.6.9.3

Answer 5.14

Answer **B** — The Misuse of Drugs Act 1971, s. 8 states:

> A person commits an offence if, being the occupier or concerned in the management of any premises, he knowingly permits or suffers any of the following activities to take place on those premises, that is to say:
> (a) producing or attempting to produce a controlled drug in contravention of section 4(1) of this Act;
> (b) supplying or attempting to supply a controlled drug to another in contravention of section 4(1) of this Act, or offering to supply a controlled drug to another in contravention of section 4(1);
> (c) preparing opium for smoking;
> (d) smoking cannabis, cannabis resin or prepared opium.

As can be seen, it applies to occupiers and not just owners; answer A is therefore incorrect. It does, however, require that it was necessary to establish that the activity of smoking had taken place and not merely that the permission had been given (*R v Auguste* (2003) *The Times*, 15 December); answer D is therefore incorrect. It is also not sufficient that the drugs and paraphernalia were present — it seems the police may have timed their raid a bit too soon as no smoking had taken place — answer C is therefore incorrect.

Crime, para. 1.6.8.10

Answer 5.15

Answer **D** — Section 1 of the Anti-social Behaviour Act 2003 deals with premises where drugs are used unlawfully:

(1) This section applies to premises if a police officer not below the rank of superintendent (the authorising officer) has reasonable grounds for believing —

    (a) that at any time during the relevant period the premises have been used in connection with the unlawful use, production or supply of a Class A controlled drug, and

    (b) that the use of the premises is associated with the occurrence of disorder or serious nuisance to members of the public.

So it's a Superintendent who authorises, not an assistant chief constable (ACC); answers A and C are incorrect. The relevant period over which the officer can consider the use of the club is also defined in the Act by s. 1(10): 'The relevant period is the period of three months ending with the day on which the authorising officer considers whether to authorise the issue of a closure notice in respect of the premises'. So three months, and not one month, is the appropriate period; answer B is therefore incorrect.

Crime, para. 1.6.8.11

Answer 5.16

Answer **B** — The secret is in the wording of the warrant: if the warrant only allows for searching of premises, that in itself will not give authority to search people on the premises unless the officer can point to some other authority allowing that search (see *Chief Constable of Thames Valley Police* v *Hepburn* [2002] *The Times*, 19 December). However, does that searching extend to everybody on the premises, even those there for an ancillary purpose? The Divisional Court has held that it is reasonable to restrict the movement of people within the premises to allow the search to be conducted properly (see *DPP* v *Meaden* (2004) *The Times*, 2 January). So the police can search the meter reader without his permission and can restrict his movements; answers A, C and D are therefore incorrect. After all, the officers only have his word that he is there to read meters (or am I cynical!)

Crime, para. 1.6.9.1

Answer 5.17

Answer **A** — Section 1 of the Anti-social Behaviour Act 2003 relates to closure notices. The police have power to close down premises being used for the supply, use or production of Class A drugs where there is associated serious nuisance or disorder. Section 4 of the Anti-social Behaviour Act 2003, which deals with offences relating to those closure notices, states:

5. Misuse of Drugs

   (1) A person commits an offence if he remains on or enters premises in contravention of a closure notice.

   (2) A person commits an offence if —

     (a) he obstructs a constable or an authorised person acting under section 1(6) or 3(2),

     (b) he remains on premises in respect of which a closure order has been made, or

     (c) he enters the premises.

There is a statutory defence courtesy of s. 4(4):

   (4) But a person does not commit an offence under subsection (1) or subsection (2)(b) or (c) if he has a reasonable excuse for entering or being on the premises (as the case may be).

Lastly the power of arrest is statutory not 'arrestable' (as per s. 24 of the Police and Criminal Evidence Act 1984) (answers C and D are incorrect):

   (5) A constable in uniform may arrest a person he reasonably suspects of committing or having committed an offence under this section.

It is a statutory power of arrest given to a constable in uniform; therefore answer B is incorrect.

Crime, para. 1.6.8.13

6 | Offences Arising out of Pregnancy and Childbirth

Please note that the questions in this chapter relate to material in the Blackstone's Police Manuals which has been excluded from the OSPRE® syllabus for 2005.

STUDY PREPARATION

Thankfully, most officers will never deal with any of the offences outlined in this chapter. Nevertheless, for the sake of completeness in covering the law relating to assaults, battery and homicide, it is important to understand how these areas fit in. The subject of abortion carries with it strong feelings and emotions. Although individual views vary greatly the legal issues are relatively clear — if not universally supported.

The coming into force of the Human Rights Act 1998 reinforced an individual's right to life, along with a positive obligation on the State to protect that right. Even though the European Court of Human Rights has made a number of clear rulings on the area of abortion, the 1998 Act may be instrumental in the development of this emotive area.

QUESTIONS

Question 6.1

STUBBS, a married woman, has been having an affair. Having missed her period she believes she may be pregnant. She does not wish her husband to find out and asks her brother, who is a pharmacist, to give her something to induce an abortion. Her brother produces a mixture with which he intends to induce an abortion and STUBBS drinks it. However, as she is not in fact pregnant, the mixture has no effect.

Has either STUBBS or her brother committed an offence under s. 58 of the Offences Against the Person Act 1861 relating to abortion?

A Full offence by STUBBS, an attempt by her brother.

B An attempt by STUBBS, full offence by her brother.

C An attempt by both as she is not pregnant.

D Neither commits any offence as she is not pregnant.

Question 6.2

AMY, who is 15 years old, secretly gives birth to a child. Desperate to hide this fact from her parents, she takes the child to the local park and hides it under a bush. The child lives for a few hours, but dies of hypothermia.

At which point, if any, does AMY commit the offence of concealing the birth?

A As soon as she forms the intention to conceal the birth.

B As soon as she hides the child in the bushes.

C As soon as the child dies.

D She does not commit this offence.

Question 6.3

THOMPSON's wife gives birth to a child, but dies during labour. THOMPSON is over-come with grief on the death of his wife and the balance of his mind is disturbed by this traumatic incident. He has not fully recovered from this when he takes the child home, and is so traumatised he blames the child for the death. THOMPSON deliber-ately does not feed or look after the child and it dies.

Is THOMPSON guilty of infanticide?

A No, as infanticide only relates to wilful acts, not omissions.

B No, the offence can only be committed by the child's mother.

C Yes, provided he can show the balance of his mind was disturbed.

D Yes, as the act allows wilful omissions to be considered.

Question 6.4

'Legal' abortion can be carried out on a pregnancy that has not exceeded what period?

A 22 weeks.

B 24 weeks.

C 26 weeks.

D 28 weeks.

Question 6.5

STRUTHERS goes to MILLS's flat in connection with a proposed abortion. There was a pan on the stove containing various instruments, which undoubtedly could be used for the purpose of procuring an abortion. MILLS stated that he was boiling the instruments to sterilize them before performing the abortion, having obtained them from his friend for such purpose.

Dealing only with supplying or procuring means for abortion under s. 59 of the Offences Against the Person Act 1861, at what point, if any, would MILLS commit the offence?

A Only if MILLS went on to use the instruments to perform the abortion.
B When he begins to sterilize the instruments for the procedure.
C When he obtains the instruments from his friend.
D When he agrees with STRUTHERS to perform the procedure.

ANSWERS

Answer 6.1

Answer **B** — The full offence is committed by a woman who *must be* pregnant, therefore answer A is incorrect. However, this is not necessary where another person is charged with the offence, and therefore answers C and D are incorrect as her brother could commit the substantive offence. As the offence is indictable, STUBBS may well be guilty of attempting the offence, even if she was acting on her own, particularly as she has clearly acted in a way that is more than merely preparatory to the commission of the substantive offence.

Crime, para. 1.7.4

Answer 6.2

Answer **D** — The accused's act must be done in relation to a dead body, so that the offence is not committed where the accused conceals a living child which later dies. As the statute says, 'secret disposition of the dead body of the said child'. Therefore, answers A, B and C are incorrect. An alternative and more appropriate charge would appear to be some form of homicide in relation to the initial act of concealing the living child which led to its death.

Crime, para. 1.7.3

Answer 6.3

Answer **B** — The offence predates the introduction of the defence of diminished responsibility and is designed to serve a similar role in relation to killings of very young children by their *mothers* in circumstances where they are not fully responsible for their actions. Answers A, C and D are therefore incorrect.

Although it does include wilful omissions, the offence does not extend to fathers traumatised by events. Here the only charge could be murder; however, a defence of diminished responsibility could be available.

Crime, para. 1.7.2

Answer 6.4

Answer **B** — There is a fixed time-limit of 24 weeks for abortions under s. 1(1)(a) of the Abortion Act 1967, but no time-limit at all (up to the point of a live birth) under s. 1(1)(b), (c) or (d). Also note that the opinion, formed in good faith, of two medical practitioners is required, except where necessary to save the life of the woman or to prevent injury to her physical or mental health. Consequently, answers A, C and D are incorrect.

Crime, para. 1.7.4.1

Answer 6.5

Answer **C** — This offence requires supply or procuring of instruments for the purpose of procuring a miscarriage of any woman; simple possession is not enough. 'Supply' means supply to another, and conversely 'procure' means procure from another, i.e. 'get possession of something of which you do not have possession already' (*R* v *Mills* [1963] 1 QB 522). The offence is complete when Mills 'procured' the instruments with knowledge of their intended use. The act of sterilizing them, or using them does not make out this offence (answers A and B are incorrect), and more than an agreement is needed (answer D is incorrect).

Crime, para. 1.7.4.2

7 Offences Against the Person

STUDY PREPARATION

This chapter deals with all non-fatal offences against the person, combining the relevant chapters of the *Blackstone's Police Manual*. This chapter examines the definition of assault and battery; it also addresses the offences of common assault, actual and grievous bodily harm, and the differences between them. Of particular importance in this area is the required element of state of mind (*mens rea*) and how that differs between offences.

Specific assaults in relation to police officers are considered, along with the less common offences of torture and poisoning. This chapter also covers the very serious offences of false imprisonment, kidnapping and hostage-taking. Although infrequently charged, these offences are perhaps of greater significance in the light of recent terrorist activity. This chapter should be read in conjunction with CPS Charging Standards.

QUESTIONS

Question 7.1

GRAHAM has been lawfully arrested for an assault where he punched a neighbour. The matter has been investigated and a charge of common assault is being laid.

What should the charge outline in relation to the offence?

A Assault and battery.

B Assault by battery.

C Assault or battery.

D Assault by beating.

Question 7.2

In considering the legal definition of assault, which of the following is correct?
A There must be intention to cause fear, although actual fear need not be proven.
B There can be recklessness as to fear caused and actual fear need not be proven.
C There must be fear of force being used, even though it may not be immediate.
D There must be fear of force being used and it must be immediate.

Question 7.3

DOUGHERTY takes her children to their dentist, WALKER. She consents to the children receiving fillings. During the procedure DOUGHERTY becomes concerned that WALKER is either drunk or drugged and reports the matter to the police. During the investigation is transpires that WALKER is taking drugs prescribed for a psychiatric illness, and for that reason he was suspended by the General Dental Council two months ago. The police are considering charging WALKER with assault.

Has WALKER unlawfully assaulted the children?
A No, DOUGHERTY has given true consent.
B No, any formal medical practice is not an assault.
C Yes, DOUGHERTY has given consent obtained by fraud.
D Yes, WALKER is suspended and no longer covered by law as it relates to consent.

Question 7.4

CHRITON stopped his car at a bus stop and told a lone women waiting for the bus that the bus had broken down about half a mile down the road (this was not in fact true). He offered the woman a lift. She accepted, but then asked to be let out of the car after a short distance. CHRITON refused and kept the woman in his car. He gets to his house and forces her down into the basement.

At what point, if any, does CHRITON 'kidnap' the woman?
A He does not kidnap her, she consents to get in the car.
B He kidnaps her when she first gets into the car.
C He kidnaps her when he refuses to let her out.
D He kidnaps her when he takes her into his house.

Question 7.5

SWALES is a store detective employed by a major retail chain. He witnesses a theft of a £200 cashmere sweater and follows the suspect, GRAINGER, outside the shop.

SWALES holds GRAINGER and asks him to return to the shop as he has items for which he has not paid. GRAINGER pulls a knife and threatens SWALES with it. SWALES backs off and GRAINGER makes good his escape.

Has GRAINGER committed an offence of assault with intent to resist arrest under s. 38 of the Offences Against the Person Act 1861?

A No, as it applies to police officers making arrests only.

B No, as it applies to assaults involving actual injury only.

C Yes, as it applies to arrests made by any citizen, not just police officers.

D Yes, provided it was proved that GRAINGER suspected he was being arrested.

Question 7.6

Constable DOUGHTY wishes to question MILLS about an alleged assault. The officer attends at MILLS's home address and tells him the nature of the incident. Knowing that he is about to be arrested, MILLS grabs hold of Constable DOUGHTY's arm and pulls him into the doorway; he then slams the door on the officer's arm and makes good his escape. As a result of this attack, Constable DOUGHTY's arm is broken in two places. When, interviewed, MILLS states that he did not intend to cause the injury, but accepts that his conduct presented a risk of some harm to the officer.

Which of the following statements is correct?

A This would not amount to a s. 18 assault, as there was no malice, i.e. premeditation.

B This would not amount to a s. 18 assault, as there was no intention to cause serious harm.

C This would amount to a s. 18 assault, as MILLS intended to prevent his lawful arrest.

D This would not amount to a s. 18 assault, as MILLS had not actually been arrested.

Question 7.7

PEARSON suspects that his wife is having an affair, as she goes out every Friday and Saturday night. She denies the allegation and intends to go out with her friends this Friday. When Friday comes, PEARSON follows her into town, goes into the club she is in, grabs hold of her and takes her back to his car about 100 metres down the road. His wife breaks free and runs back to her friends.

Has PEARSON committed the offence of kidnapping?

A No, as he only took her a short way.

B No, you cannot kidnap your spouse.

C   No, he commits the offence of false imprisonment.

D   Yes, all the elements of the offence are met.

Question 7.8

REES has had enough of her neighbour PATEY playing loud music at all hours of the day and night. One morning she took PATEY's milk from his doorstep. REES crushed eight sleeping tablets prescribed for her own use and put them in the milk, returning the bottle to PATEY's doorstep. REES knew exactly what she was doing and intended to make PATEY ill. The effects of the tablets were reduced by the milk, however, and they simply made PATEY fall asleep.

Has REES committed the offence of poisoning with intent under s. 24 of the Offences Against the Person Act 1861?

A   Yes, as REES intended to injure, aggrieve or annoy PATEY.

B   No, as the drugs are not 'noxious things'.

C   Yes, provided that REES was at least reckless to any injury caused.

D   No, as PATEY's life was never in danger.

Question 7.9

VICKERY is the Mayor of a small town and a strong advocate of European monetary union. Whilst leaving the town hall he sees STROUD writing graffiti on the front door. It stated, 'you can stick your Euros up your arse Vickery'. Incensed at this criminal damage, VICKERY makes a citizen's arrest and takes his prisoner back up into his office. In there he makes STROUD squat in the corner of his office and leaves him there for an hour. VICKERY then asks all 15 members of staff to come into the room at look at STROUD. They all laugh at him causing him extreme humiliation. VICKERY calls the police and STROUD is arrested for criminal damage.

Which of the following statements is true?

A   VICKERY has not committed torture, as there was no real physical suffering by STROUD.

B   VICKERY has not committed torture, as he is not acting in the performance of his public duties.

C   VICKERY has committed torture, as he is a public official and has subjected STROUD to degrading treatment.

D   VICKERY and his staff members have all committed torture.

Question 7.10

TURNER has fallen out with his girlfriend following a heated argument. He sees her in town one afternoon with another man. TURNER's girlfriend is carrying her two-year-old son. TURNER punches his girlfriend on the nose, breaking it and making it bleed. At the time she is punched she drops the child, causing cuts and bruises to his face. TURNER then threatens his girlfriend's friend, who, fearing for his immediate safety, runs off.

In relation to this action, on whom has TURNER committed battery?

A His girlfriend and her friend.

B Only his girlfriend.

C Both his girlfriend and the child.

D All three of them.

Question 7.11

STEVENS is having an argument with BRIDGES in the street, opposite the police station. BRIDGES picks up a large piece of wood and raises it above his head. He says to STEVENS, 'How dare you swear at me. If we weren't opposite the nick I'd let you have this'.

Which of the following statements is correct?

A BRIDGES has committed an assault as he threatened to use immediate force.

B BRIDGES has committed an assault as he picked up a weapon.

C BRIDGES has not committed an assault as force was not actually used.

D BRIDGES has not committed an assault as his threat was negated by his words.

Question 7.12

FAULKNER is a Police Community Support Officer (PCSO) employed by her local Police Authority. Whilst on patrol she meets DALTON, who takes exception to her presence and wrestles her to the ground. CONNIKIE, a member of the public and very community minded, tries to pull DALTON off of FAULKNER and DALTON responds by pushing CONNIKIE over.

Which of the following is true in relation to the Police Reform Act 2002?

A DALTON has committed an offence of assaulting a designated or accredited person in relation to both FAULKNER and CONNIKIE and is arrestable.

B DALTON has committed an offence of assaulting a designated or accredited person in relation to FAULKNER only and is arrestable.

C DALTON has committed an offence of assaulting a designated or accredited person in relation to both FAULKNER and CONNIKIE, and there is no power of arrest.

D DALTON has committed an offence of assaulting a designated or accredited person in relation to FAULKNER only, and there is no power of arrest.

Question 7.13

Constable RICHLEY is a black officer. She is making an arrest for a public order offence when the suspect pushes her to the ground, saying 'fuck you black bitch, get back to the jungle where you belong'. Constable RICHLEY is hurt but her injuries do not amount to a s. 47 assault.

The behaviour demonstrated by the offender amounts to racial or religious hatred. In relation to that, which of the following is true?

A In these circumstances the offender can *only* be charged with assault on police or assault with intent to resist arrest.

B The offender cannot be charged with a racially aggravated assault as this only applies to at least a s. 47 offence.

C The offender can be arrested (s. 24, PACE) and charged with racially aggravated common assault.

D The offender can be charged with racially aggravated common assault, but there is no power of arrest.

Question 7.14

FARQUASON is infected with the HIV virus, and has unprotected sex with a woman he met in a nightclub. The woman consents fully to have sex with FARQUASON, and it was her idea not to use a condom. She contracts HIV as a direct result of this sexual encounter with FARQUASON.

Has FARQUASON committed an offence under s. 20 the Offences Against the Person Act 1861?

A Yes, in these circumstances the offence is made out.

B Yes, provided the prosecution can show that FARQUASON had the relevant intent.

C No, as the woman should have been aware of the risk of having unprotected sex.

D No, as the woman consented to have sex and to have it unprotected.

ANSWERS

Answer 7.1

Answer **D** — The Divisional Court in *DPP* v *Taylor* [1992] QB 645 has held that all common assaults and batteries are now offences under s. 39 of the Criminal Justice Act 1988, and that the information must include a reference to that section. An information would be bad for duplicity if the phrase 'assault and battery' were used, which makes answers A, B and C all incorrect; the court suggested that 'assault by beating' was the appropriate wording. This advice has been given to all forces by the CPS, who recommend that wording as the most appropriate for the charge.

Crime, para. 1.8.2.2

Answer 7.2

Answer **D** — There has to be intentional or reckless causation of the fear of force, but the fear of force is the key to assault, which makes answers A and B incorrect. An assault requires conduct which causes the victim to apprehend the immediate use of unlawful force upon him. The concept of immediacy has nevertheless been interpreted with some flexibility, and there have been a number of recent cases in which 'stalkers' have been prosecuted for assault on that basis. In *Smith* v *Chief Superintendent, Woking Police Station* (1983) 76 Cr App R 234, the Divisional Court held that a threat of violence could be considered immediate, even though the accused was still outside the victim's home, looking in at her through a window, and would have needed to force an entry before he could attack her. This, however, relates to the time period and not the victim's actual fear, which remains as the fear of immediate use of unlawful force, and therefore answer C is incorrect.

Crime, paras 1.8.2.4, 1.8.2.5

Answer 7.3

Answer **A** — This question deals with consent and broadly follows the outline of the circumstances in the case of *R* v *Richardson* [1999] QB 444. In that case it was held that a dentist's failure to inform patients that the General Dental Council had suspended him did not affect the true 'consent' given for medical treatment (answer D is incorrect). In *Richardson*, Otton LJ held that there had been no deception as to the identity of the dentist, or the nature of the act carried out, and this therefore could not vitiate consent and there could be no assault. Consent obtained by fraud would relate to the identity of the dentist as a trained dentist, which is not the case here, and answer C is therefore incorrect. Consent to medical treatment is true consent, but going beyond agreed treatment could be an assault, e.g. the indecent touching of the patient, and thus answer B is incorrect.

Crime, para. 1.8.2.6

Answer 7.4

Answer **B** — Kidnapping is defined at common law as 'the taking or carrying away of one person by another without the consent of the person so taken or carried away, and without lawful excuse'.

The issue here is consent, and certainly the woman consents to get into the car. However, the Court of Appeal held in *R v Cort* [2003] 3 WLR 1300, that if the consent is obtained by fraud, as it was here through the lies told, then this would not be true consent. Without such consent, the offence is made out when the woman gets in the car and, as CHRITON has kidnapped her, answer A is incorrect. Although he further detains her, this is more the offence of false imprisonment, and happens after she is kidnapped; answers C and D are therefore incorrect.

Crime, para. 1.9.5

Answer 7.5

Answer **C** — On a literal reading of s. 38 of the Offences Against the Person Act 1861, the only *actus reus* required is that of common assault, making answer B incorrect, whereas the *mens rea* is that of common assault, coupled with an intent to resist or prevent one's own, or another person's, lawful arrest or detention. Nevertheless, it is firmly established that the arrest or detention in question must in fact be lawful (*R v Self* [1992] 3 All ER 476; *R v Lee* [2000] Crim LR 991) and this is an essential element. The person making the arrest (or trying to) need not be a police officer, which makes answer A incorrect. It may be a private citizen assisting such an officer, or a private citizen or store detective making a 'citizen's arrest'.

The accused has no defence if his mistake is merely one of law, as for example where he does not appreciate that a citizen has a power of arrest, or where he assumes that an arrest is unlawful merely because he is (or believes himself to be) innocent of the offence in question. This makes answer D incorrect.

Crime, para. 1.8.3.2

Answer 7.6

Answer **C** — 'Maliciously' does not need premeditation but rather amounts to subjective recklessness, and the suspect admits this. He accepts that there was a risk of harm. He does not have to foresee the degree of harm and therefore answer A is incorrect. This offence has two strands:

- An intention to cause serious harm; *or*
- An intention to resist or prevent lawful apprehension.

Where, in contrast, it is alleged that the defendant merely intended to resist arrest etc., malice becomes an important further element to be proved, and therefore answer B is incorrect. It applies to intention to prevent as well as resist arrest, and not just when someone has actually been arrested, and therefore D is incorrect.

Crime, para. 1.8.4.3

Answer 7.7

Answer **D** — The offences of false imprisonment, kidnapping and hostage-taking are very closely linked, in fact the state of mind required is the same. In *R v Rahman* (1985) 81 Cr App R 349, it was stated that the *mens rea* for false imprisonment is intentional or reckless restraint of a person's movement (recklessness here means subjective recklessness). Answer C is incorrect, as PEARSON has not restrained his wife's movement. You can kidnap your spouse, as you could kidnap any person, provided the basic definition of the offence is met (*R v Reid* [1973] QB 299) and therefore answer B is incorrect. Also, the distance taken may only be a short one (*R v Wellard* [1978] 3 All ER 161) and therefore answer A is incorrect.

Crime, paras 1.9.5, 1.9.7

Answer 7.8

Answer **A** — The offence is one of specific intent, and recklessness is not sufficient, so answer C is incorrect. In *R v Marcus* [1981] 2 All ER 833, the Court of Appeal held that a substance which might be harmless in small quantities could therefore be 'noxious' if the quantity administered was sufficient to injure, aggrieve or annoy (answer B is incorrect). Section 24 is distinguished from s. 23 of the 1861 Act, in that the latter requires proof of a consequence — namely, the endangering of a person's life or the infliction of grievous bodily harm — and therefore answer D is incorrect.

Crime, paras 1.9.3, 1.9.3.1

Answer 7.9

Answer **B** — VICKERY does not appear to be acting in the performance or purported performance of his duties, and therefore cannot be guilty of torture (answer C is incorrect). It might be argued that he saw his actions as being part of his civic managerial duties, but this is unlikely to succeed. The meaning of 'severe pain or suffering' does not have to amount to grievous bodily harm, actual bodily harm or any standard measured by degree of injury. Indeed, the wording of s. 134(3) of the Criminal Justice Act 1988 provides that the pain or suffering may be purely mental. It is the severity of the pain rather than whether or not identifiable injury results that should be considered, though evidence of injury would be admissible evidence of the severity of the pain. Answer A is therefore incorrect. The arguments against the actions of VICKERY falling within the scope of his public duties apply even more clearly to the actions of his staff, and therefore answer D is also incorrect.

Crime, para. 1.9.2

Answer 7.10

Answer **C** — A battery requires the unlawful application of force upon the victim, so, although the male friend has been assaulted, he has not been 'battered'. Answers A and D are therefore wrong. Where someone strikes another causing her to drop and injure her child, it has been held to be a battery against both (*Haystead* v *Chief Constable of Derbyshire* [2000] 3 All ER 890). As the child has also been assaulted, answer B is incorrect.

Crime, para. 1.8.2.2

Answer 7.11

Answer **D** — Words used by the accused may indicate that no real attack is imminent, even where the circumstances might suggest otherwise. This principle has been clearly established since the very ancient case of *Tuberville* v *Savage* (1669) 1 Mod 3, where, in the course of a quarrel with S, T placed his hand on the hilt of his sword (an act which might ordinarily have been construed as an assault) and exclaimed, 'If it were not assize time, I would not take such language from you'. 'Assize time' meant that the judges were in town, and no doubt T feared being arrested and tried. The same principle applies on the facts of this question where BRIDGES makes a 'qualified' threat to STEVENS (answers A and B are therefore incorrect). As a point of interest the older the case law the better law it is, as it has stood the test of time, over 330 years in this case! There can be assault where no force is used, i.e. threats making the other person fear immediate attack, and therefore answer C is incorrect.

Crime, para. 1.8.2.2

Answer 7.12

Answer **C** — The Police Reform Act 2002, s. 46(1) states:

(1) Any person who assaults —
   (a) a designated person in the execution of his duty
   (b) an accredited person in the execution of his duty
   (c) a person assisting a designated or accredited person in the execution of his duty
   is guilty of an offence.

Provided the designated or accredited person was acting in the execution of his or her duty, it is an offence to assault either that person or anyone assisting him or her, therefore answers B and D are incorrect. There is, however, no specific power of arrest, therefore answer A is incorrect.

Crime, para. 1.8.3.5

Answer 7.13

Answer **D** — Although the offences of assault on police (s. 89 of the Police Act 1996) and assault with intent to resist arrest (s. 38 of the Offences Against the Person Act 1861) are perfectly valid for this instance, given the racially aggravated factors a more serious charge is appropriate. Also answer A also says can *only* be charged, precluding any other offence such as common assault, which is not true, and for that reason answer A is incorrect. In *R* v *Jacobs* [2001] 2 Cr App R (S) 174, a female police officer was subjected to repeated verbal racial abuse by a female suspect who had been arrested and taken to the police station. Bennett J commented that 'police officers are entitled to be protected, just as any other members of the public, from racial abuse'. And the Crime and Disorder Act 1998 extends this racially aggravating factor to various levels of assault, common assault being one of them (s. 29(1)(c) of the 1998 Act), therefore answer B is incorrect. This aggravating feature to the assault makes common assault an either way offence and increases the penalty from 6 months' to 2 years' imprisonment on indictment. It does not, however, give a specific power of arrest; answer C is therefore incorrect.

Crime, para. 1.8.3.1

Answer 7.14

Answer **A** — Section 20 of the Offences Against the Person Act 1861 does not require intent to commit grievous bodily harm (GBH), that is a s.18 offence, and the prosecution only have to show that the accused unlawfully and maliciously inflicted GBH, therefore answer B is incorrect. Certainly contracting HIV could be said to be an 'injury resulting in some permanent disability' and as such amounts to GBH; the issue here is consent. In *R v Dica* [2004] EWCA Crim 1103, it was held that recklessness to consent, as such, was not in issue. In *Dica* the defendant had unprotected sex with two women, knowing he was HIV positive. Although both women were willing to have sexual intercourse with the defendant, the prosecution's case was that their agreement would never have been given if they had known of the defendant's condition. The defendant stated that he told both women of his condition, and that they were nonetheless willing to have sexual intercourse with him. However, the judge ruled that whether or not the complainants knew of the defendant's condition, their consent, if any, was irrelevant and provided no defence, since *R v Brown* [1994] 1 AC 212 deprived the complainants of the legal capacity to consent to such serious harm. In *Brown* it was held that sado-masochistic acts which occurred in private and which were consented to could found charges under the 1861 Act, ss. 20 and 47, if the injuries, though not permanent, were neither transient nor trifling. So, irrespective of the victim's willingness to place herself at risk, or to consent to sexual activity, FARQUASON has committed the offence; answer C and D are therefore incorrect.

Crime, paras 1.8.2.6, 1.8.4.2

8 | Sexual Offences

STUDY PREPARATION

Sexual offences cover a wide range of activities. In answering these questions there is a real need first of all to identify who is doing what to whom. Usually the key to the offences that arise from such activities is to be found in:

- the ages of the parties;
- the intent of the offender;
- the consent of the victim;
- the accompanying circumstances.

Until recently sexual offences were subject to an Act almost half a century old—ask yourself, have sexual activity and attitudes changed since then? The existing framework was described as 'archaic, incoherent and discriminatory'. The resulting Sexual Offences Act 2003 is a landmark statute that repeals almost all of the Sexual Offences Act 1956 and many other statutory provisions enacted since, delivering, in effect, a new criminal code of sexual offences. The Sexual Offences Act 2003 not only introduces a considerable number of new offences and criminalises certain types of conduct not previously subjected to the written law, it also substantially redefines many sex crimes, incorporating new terms and language deemed more appropriate to contemporary society.

QUESTIONS

Question 8.1

FERGUSON met a girl at a party and she agreed to go back to his house. At FERGUSON'S house the girl agrees to have sexual intercourse with him, and they both consume a lot of alcohol; the girl is very drunk. FERGUSON goes to the bathroom, and prior to his return the girl falls asleep on the bed. FERGUSON has sex with her while she sleeps.

Has FERGUSON committed rape?

A No as she agreed to sex prior to falling asleep.

B No, as her drunkenness was self-induced.

C Yes, even although she earlier agreed.

D Yes, but only if the prosecution prove lack of real consent.

Question 8.2

JENKINSON is sexually attracted to his male colleague, COLLINS. One night JENKINSON persuades COLLINS to go back to his house, where he thinks he will be able to have sex with him; and to ensure sex takes place, JENKINSON plies COLLINS with alcohol and adds drugs to the drink to stupefy COLLINS. COLLINS becomes all but unconscious; JENKINSON then has oral sexual intercourse with him.

What offence, if any, has JENKINSON committed?

A Rape.

B Assault by penetration.

C Administering a substance with intent.

D Causing a person to engage in sexual activity without consent.

Question 8.3

DAWSON, a woman, is lying in the local park one summer's day. Feeling aroused, she begins to masturbate herself, openly, and the park is very busy. Several people walk by and see DAWSON; her vagina is clearly visible, but no one is offended by this behaviour. DAWSON was only intending self-pleasure.

Has DAWSON committed the offence of exposure?

A Yes, as she exposed her genitals in public.

B Yes, as she exposed her genitals in public and people can see her.

C No, as no one was offended by the behaviour.

D No, as she did not intend anyone to be caused alarm or distress.

Question 8.4

BRIAN is 15 years of age, but is a mature boy who looks older than he is. He has been infatuated with his neighbour's 25-year-old daughter for some time, and wishes to have sex with her. One night they are alone in BRIAN's house and he starts to seduce her; she freely consents. They do not have sexual intercourse, but she masturbates BRIAN.

Which of the following is correct?

A The woman has committed a sexual assault.

B The woman has committed an offence of sexual activity with a child.

C The woman has committed no offence, as the boy consented to the act.

D The woman has committed no offence, as no intercourse took place.

Question 8.5

STRUTHERS and his girlfriend, who are both 17 years of age, are in their bedroom and are joined by STRUTHERS' younger brother, who is 13 years of age. Whilst the brother watches, STRUTHERS and his girlfriend participate in mutual masturbation and oral sex. They both know the child is present, and both are getting sexual gratification from the fact they are being watched by the brother. The brother is not offended and enjoys watching.

Is this engaging in sexual activity in the presence of a child?

A Yes, as they are over 17 years of age.

B Yes, because the brother is under 14 years of age.

C No, because they are not 18 years of age or over.

D No, because the child is not offended, nor forced to watch.

Question 8.6

GUNN invites DAVIES, who is 19 and suffering from a severe mental disorder, back to his house. GUNN then asks DAVIES to take all his clothes off, which he willingly does. Because of his mental disorder DAVIES is unable to refuse involvement in sexual activity. GUNN then tries to penetrate DAVIES anally, which DAVIES has freely agreed to. GUNN only just manages to penetrate DAVIES, then gives up and sends DAVIES home.

In order to prove the offence of sexual activity with a person with a mental disorder (s. 30), what does the prosecution have to show?

A That GUNN knew DAVIES suffered from a mental disorder.

B That GUNN knew DAVIES suffered from a mental disorder and knew he was unlikely to refuse his advances.

C That GUNN used inducements to get DAVIES to agree to the touching.

D That GUNN coerced DAVIES into agreeing to the touching.

Question 8.7

What is the minimum period for which a risk of sexual harm order (RSHO) may be made?

A Two years.

B Three years.

C Five years.

D Indefinite.

Question 8.8

STEPHENSON, 22 years old, is a convicted child sex offender currently on parole. He is seen by concerned parents every day of the week standing outside a local primary school. He does or says nothing, but is always outside the school when the children are released.

What is the fullest extent to which a risk of sexual harm order (RSHO) may be made to protect children?

A To protect all the children at the school who are at risk from STEPHENSON.

B To protect a particular child at the school who is at risk from STEPHENSON.

C To protect any child in the locality who is at risk from STEPHENSON.

D To protect any child anywhere who is at risk from STEPHENSON.

Question 8.9

YOUNG lives with his prostitute girlfriend and has recently encouraged her to go to work as a prostitute for DIBLEY, a local drug dealer. YOUNG hopes that in providing his girlfriend, DIBLEY will supply him with cheap drugs in the future, which is likely. YOUNG receives no money from DIBLEY for the deal. His girlfriend is happy with this arrangement, as she will make more money working for DIBLEY.

Has YOUNG committed an offence of controlling prostitution for gain under s. 53 of the Sexual Offences Act 2003?

A No, there has been no gain as yet, only future hopes of gain.

B No, as YOUNG's girlfriend is not forced into prostitution.

C Yes, as there will be future financial advantage.

D Yes, as the prostitute will make money and she lives with YOUNG.

Question 8.10

MARKS and his female secretary, HIRST, attended a conference in Blackpool. While they were there, MARKS tried to get HIRST to have sex with him. She refused and MARKS got angry. He told her that if she didn't have sex with him, he would beat her husband up with a hammer when they got back home. Fearing for her husband's safety, HIRST had sex with MARKS. In fact MARKS had no intention of harming her husband.

Has MARKS committed rape?

A Yes, as MARKS threatened violence against HIRST's husband.

B Yes, as HIRST only consented through MARKS' deception.

C No, as the violence threatened was not immediate.

D No, as the violence threatened was not against HIRST.

Question 8.11

BROADHURST and his girlfriend LAWRENCE are having anal sex in a toilet cubicle in a mens toilet. Another man enters the toilet and hears what he clearly believes to be a couple having sex; he laughs and leaves the toilet.

Regarding sexual activity in a public lavatory, which of the following is true?

A This offence is not made out because no one was offended or disgusted.

B This offence is not made out as they are not engaged in homosexual sex.

C This offence is made out only because it involves anal sex.

D This offence is made out and both are guilty of it.

Question 8.12

PEARD was given a caution for being a common prostitute, and asks you if she can dispute the interpretation of her actions as being 'soliciting'.

Which of the following is correct?

A No, she cannot dispute the caution, as it is not an official caution for an offence.

B No, she cannot dispute the caution, as it is only recorded in a police held register.

C Yes, she can apply to a court within 7 days of the caution.

D Yes, she can apply to a court within 14 days of the caution.

Question 8.13

TURNER is a convicted paedophile, and notified police of his home address. He has stayed with a friend some 300 miles from his home address; he stayed with this friend for 3 days, 2 months ago, and now intends spending another 3 days with him. He has not notified police of the address of his friend.

Should he now notify police that he is staying with his friend?

A No, as he is not staying there for 7 days.

B No, as he has not stayed there for 7 days in the last year.

C Yes, he must notify police of any place he is staying, for any period.

D Yes, he is away from his notified address for more than 2 days.

Question 8.14

BAKER is a man who wishes to pay a prostitute for sexual intercourse. He has never done this before and is a bit unsure what to do. He gets into his car and drives to a residential area he believes, mistakenly, to be a well-known red light area. He notices a lone woman standing near the bus stop; he stops beside her and says 'Are you doing business?'. Not knowing what he means she says 'No I'm waiting for a bus, what sort of business are you looking for?' Confused, BAKER drives straight home.

Which of the following is correct?

A He has committed an offence of kerb-crawling as his behaviour is likely to cause annoyance to the woman.

B He has committed an offence of kerb-crawling as he has solicited the woman from his car.

C He has not committed an offence of kerb-crawling as the woman was not offended.

D He has not committed an offence of kerb-crawling as he did not intend to cause annoyance to the woman.

Question 8.15

CLINTON has a 15-year-old daughter, KAREN, who looks older than her age. CLINTON introduced KAREN to his friend, GEORGE, who is a pimp. Between them, CLINTON and GEORGE persuaded KAREN to become a prostitute. She agreed and went out with GEORGE on weekends only, and solicited in the street for prostitution. KAREN's mother was aware of what was happening to her daughter and encouraged her, but refused to accept any money from what the child earned.

In relation to offences under s. 48 of the Sexual Offences Act 2003 of causing or inciting child prostitution, which of the following is true?

A GEORGE has committed the offence, but CLINTON has not.

B CLINTON has committed the offence, but GEORGE has not.

C CLINTON and GEORGE have committed the offence in these circumstances.

D CLINTON, GEORGE and the child's mother have committed the offence.

Question 8.16

PORTER downloaded some pornographic pictures of children under the age of 16 from the Internet. He took them to work and lent them to his friend, WILLIS, who returned them the next day.

Who, if either, has committed an offence in relation to the photographs?

A Both: PORTER for possessing and distributing photographs; WILLIS for being in possession of them.

B Only PORTER, for possessing and distributing the photographs to another person.

C Both PORTER and WILLIS for possession, as photographs cannot be distributed to just one person in this way.

D Both PORTER and WILLIS for possession, as the offence of distributing does not include lending.

Question 8.17

PAVETT is a woman employed as a cleaner at an NHS hospital specialising in mental health. She is sexually very active and is caught one morning having sexual intercourse with a male patient, who was receiving treatment for a mental disorder at the hospital as an outpatient. The man is a regular outpatient, and PAVETT frequently sees him on a daily basis. Consider s. 39 of the Sexual Offences Act 2003, on care workers causing or inciting sexual activity.

In relation to PAVETT's actions, which of the following is correct?

A She has committed this offence as she is a care worker.

B She has committed the offence: even though she is not a care worker, the man is an outpatient.

C She has not committed the offence as she is not a care worker.

D She has not committed the offence because the man is an outpatient.

Question 8.18

COLLINS is very keen to have sexual intercourse with BETTY. She tells him she is only interested in his friendship and wants nothing more than that. One night COLLINS decides that she will have sex with him if he forces the issue, so he hides outside her bedroom window on the ledge, intent on entering and having sex with BETTY. He intends to force her to have sex, although he honestly believes she wants to. He breaks the window and enters the house. She is, however, not in the house.

Which of the following is true in relation to the Sexual Offences Act 2003, regarding COLLINS' intent?

A COLLINS commits an offence when he breaks the bedroom window.

B COLLINS commits an offence when he hides outside the bedroom window.

C COLLINS does not commit an offence, as he has an honest belief and no sex took place.

D COLLINS does not commit an offence, as Betty was not in the house.

Question 8.19

WISE, aged 48 years, owns a sweet shop, which he uses to further his paedophilic desires. He sees BEN, who is 12 years old, in the shop and has desires to touch him sexually. He arranges to meet BEN later in the local park. He has never met BEN before. He walks to the park at about 7 p.m., and meets BEN by the swings. BEN realises something is wrong and runs off before WISE can touch him.

At what point, if any, does WISE commit an offence under s. 15 of the Sexual Offences Act 2003, on child grooming?

A When he arranges to meet the child.

B When he starts walking to meet the child.

C When he first meets the child in the park.

D He does not commit the offence as he has not previously communicated with the child.

Question 8.20

GIBBONS is a biology teacher at the local High School, and SIAN is a 16-year-old pupil in his class. They are very friendly and SIAN adores GIBBONS, and they converse frequently in an Internet chatroom. GIBBONS sends indecent still photographs in an e-mail to SIAN's school computer terminal from his; they are very explicit pictures. SIAN loves the pictures and is not in the least concerned by them. GIBBONS receives sexual gratification from knowing that SIAN looks at the pictures, and if questioned by the school he will say it is part of a sex education programme.

Has GIBBONS committed an offence under s. 19 of the Sexual Offences Act 2003 on abuse of position of trust causing a child to watch a sexual act?

A Yes, but only because SIAN is a pupil in his class.
B Yes, but only because of the sexual gratification he gets.
C No, this offence only applies to a child under 16 years of age.
D No, because they are still pictures and not a 'moving image'.

Question 8.21

Section 46 of the Children Act 1989, deals with the protection of children in certain situations. In relation to the section, which of the following statements is correct?

A A constable or social worker may remove a child to suitable accommodation.
B A constable in uniform may remove a child to suitable accommodation.
C A constable may only remove a child to a police station or hospital.
D A constable may remove a child to suitable accommodation.

Question 8.22

CORNELIOUS runs a fitness club, which has many female members. He has installed a webcam in the women's changing rooms, and regularly broadcasts from his website pictures of the activities in the changing rooms. None of the women in the changing room knows about the webcam. CORNELIOUS does not watch it himself, nor does he find it sexually satisfying. CORNELIOUS does, however, sell the broadcast to persons he knows receive extreme sexual gratification from watching.

Is this voyeurism?

A Yes, but only because the women are not aware of the webcam.
B Yes, as those watching it get sexual gratification from doing so.
C No, as CORNELIOUS gets no sexual gratification from broadcasting it.
D No, as CORNELIOUS does not watch the webcam himself.

Question 8.23

TURNER has been convicted of possessing indecent photographs of a child, and has changed his home address since being released from prison, having served his sentence.

How should this notification of change of address be made?

A Must be personally at the police station.
B Can be by sending written notification.

C Can be by sending written notification or by telephoning the station.

D Must be by written notification.

Question 8.24

A Sexual Offences Prevention Order is made with a view to prohibiting a defendant from doing 'anything' described in that order.

To what sort of activity does this 'anything' apply?

A Any criminal activity relating to his previous convictions.

B Any criminal activity; the person does not have to have previous convictions.

C Any criminal activity or civil wrong; the person does not have to have previous convictions.

D Any criminal activity or civil wrong.

Question 8.25

What power exists to deal with an offender who fails to comply with notification requirements, under s. 91 of the Sexual Offences Act 2003?

A Statutory power of arrest under the 2003 Act.

B Statutory power of arrest under the 2003 Act, constable in uniform.

C Arrestable offence.

D Summary only offence, no power of arrest, report for summons.

ANSWERS

Answer 8.1

Answer **C** — The Sexual Offences Act 2003 still has consent as a key issue in rape. 'Consent' is defined by s. 74 as follows: 'For the purposes of this Part, a person consents if he agrees by choice, and has the freedom and capacity to make that choice.'

Sections 75 and 76 of the 2003 Act apply to rape, and s. 75 provides for presumptions that the person did not, in certain circumstances, consent *per se*:

(2) The circumstances are that —

    (a) any person was, at the time of the relevant act or immediately before it began, using violence against the complainant or causing the complainant to fear that immediate violence would be used against him;

    (b) any person was, at the time of the relevant act or immediately before it began, causing the complainant to fear that violence was being used, or that immediate violence would be used, against another person;

    (c) the complainant was, and the defendant was not, unlawfully detained at the time of the relevant act;

    (d) the complainant was asleep or otherwise unconscious at the time of the relevant act . . .

This means that as the girl was asleep when intercourse took place, and FERGUSON knew she was asleep, the complainant will be presumed not to have consented to the act and the defendant will be presumed not to have reasonably believed that the complainant consented.

Answer A is incorrect because, even though earlier consent was given, at the time of the act consent was presumed absent, even though the girl's condition was due to self-intoxication (which also makes answer B incorrect). This places an evidential burden upon the defendant, and not the prosecution, which makes answer D incorrect. The judge must be satisfied that the defendant can produce 'sufficient evidence' to justify putting the issue of consent before a jury; lack of such evidence will result in a direction to the jury to find the defendant guilty.

Crime, paras 1.10.3, 1.10.3.3

Answer 8.2

Answer **A** — Again this relates to consent, and s. 75(f) states:

any person had administered to or caused to be taken by the complainant, without the complainant's consent, a substance which, having regard to when it was administered or taken, was capable of causing or enabling the complainant to be stupefied or overpowered at the time of the relevant act.

This being the case, and the accused knowing that it is the case, presumes lack of consent and the offence is made out. Note that rape now includes intentionally penetrating the mouth of another person. Assault by penetration does not include the mouth, and therefore answer B is incorrect. Administering a substance with intent is a preparatory offence, i.e. date rape drugs; once the sexual act is performed, rape is the appropriate charge and answer C is therefore incorrect. Causing a person to engage in sexual activity without consent requires some other person being forced into committing a sexual act (i.e. if JENKINSON had forced COLLINS to masturbate him), answer D is therefore incorrect.

Crime, paras 1.10.3, 1.10.3.3

Answer 8.3

Answer **D** — Section 66 of the 2003 Act makes it an offence for a person intentionally to expose his or her genitals where he or she intends that someone will see them and be caused alarm or distress. It requires more than simple public display, therefore answer A is incorrect; and it is not necessary for the defendant's genitals to have been seen by anyone, so answer B is therefore incorrect. Even had no one been caused alarm or distress, the offence would be made out with the relevant intention of the offender, so answer C is therefore incorrect.

Crime, para. 1.10.8.1

Answer 8.4

Answer **B** — Section 9 of the Sexual Offences Act 2003 makes it an offence for a person aged 18 or over intentionally to engage in sexual touching of a child under 16. Whether or not the child consented to the sexual activity is irrelevant, so answer C is therefore incorrect; but this is not the case in sexual assaults where lack of consent must be established, so answer A in therefore incorrect. 'Touching' is defined by s. 79(8) of the 2003 Act and basically covers all forms of physical contact, including penetration. You must also understand what is meant by 'sexual', and s. 78 defines it. Subsection (a) covers activity that the reasonable person would always consider to be sexual because of its nature; this may be sexual intercourse, but may also be masturbation. Subsection (b) covers activity that the reasonable person would consider, because of its nature, may or may not be sexual, depending on the circumstances, or the intentions of the person carrying it out or both: for example, digital penetration of the vagina may be sexual, or may be carried out for a medical reason. Provided the reasonable person views the activity as sexual then full intercourse does not have to be shown, so answer D is therefore incorrect.

Crime, para. 1.10.5.1

Answer 8.5

Answer **C** — Section 11 makes it an offence for a person aged 18 or over intentionally to engage in sexual activity when a child under 16 is present, or in a place from which he can be observed by the child, the purpose of which is for obtaining sexual gratification from the presence of the child. 'Sexual' is defined by s. 78. The offence is met where the child is under 16 years of age, therefore answer B is incorrect; and is committed by those who are aged 18 or over, therefore answer A is incorrect. The offence is committed even where the child apparently consents to watching the sexual act, and does not need to cause offence; answer D is therefore incorrect.

This offence is intended to cover the situation where someone seeks sexual gratification not from the sexual act itself, but rather from the fact that he is performing that act in the presence or intended presence of a child. The motive of sexual gratification is a necessary safeguard intended to avoid capturing those who engage in sexual activity in front of a child for a legitimate reason. For example, a teacher who sexually kisses his partner just outside the school gates could be deemed to be engaging in sexual activity intentionally in front of a child, and might otherwise be caught by the offence.

Crime, para. 1.10.5.2

Answer 8.6

Answer **B** — Sections 30 to 33 of the Act deal with offences where the victim is unable to refuse to engage in or to watch a sexual activity because of, or for a reason related to, a mental disorder. It is a requirement of these offences that the offender knew, or could reasonably have been expected to know, that the victim had a mental disorder *and* that because of it he was likely to be unable to refuse. Note the *and*, which means that both elements of the offender's guilty knowledge have to be shown, therefore answer A is incorrect. Section 30 makes it an offence intentionally to touch someone sexually when that person, because of, or for a reason related to, a mental disorder is unable to refuse. The s. 78 definition of 'sexual' applies, and touching means all physical contact, including touching with any part of the body, with anything else and through anything, for example, through clothing. It includes penetration (s. 78(9)). Using inducements and/or threats and deceptions are separate offences in themselves (ss. 34 to 37) and are not requirements for this offence; answers C and D are therefore incorrect.

Crime, para. 1.10.7.2

Answer 8.7

Answer **A** — The Risk of Sexual Harm Order (RSHO) is a new civil preventative order which was introduced by the Sexual Offences Act 2003. RSHOs will be available in England, Wales and Northern Ireland. The RSHO is designed to protect children aged under 16 (17 in Northern Ireland) from sexual harm by adults. It is known that some abusers try to prepare children for sexual activity by exposing them to sexually explicit language or images. The RSHO is intended to help the police to prevent such behaviour.

A chief officer of police will be able to apply for, and a court will be able to make, a RSHO in respect of a person aged 18 or over where it appears he or she has, on at least two occasions, either,

(a) engaged in sexual activity involving a child or in the presence of a child;
(b) caused or incited a child to watch a person engage in sexual activity or to look at a moving or still image that is sexual;
(c) given a child anything that relates to sexual activity or contains a reference to such activity;
(d) communicated with a child, where any part of the communication is sexual;

and a RSHO is necessary to protect a child (or children) from sexual harm from the defendant (s. 123(3) of the Sexual Offences Act 2003).

An application for an order will be by complaint to a magistrates' court. The behaviour on which the application for a RSHO is based need not amount, in itself, to a criminal offence and the defendant does not need to have a previous conviction for a sexual (or any other) offence.

A RSHO may prohibit the defendant from doing anything which is necessary to protect a particular child, a group of children or children in general from sexual harm. The order will last for a fixed period of at least *2 years*, or until further notice.

As can be seen, the minimum period is 2 years, therefore answers B, C and D are incorrect.

Crime, para. 1.10.10.24

Answer 8.8

Answer **D** — The legislation states that a risk of sexual harm order (RSHO) may prohibit the defendant from doing anything which is necessary to protect a particular child, a group of children or children in general from sexual harm. It goes beyond a risk to any child or all of the children that go to the school, so answers A and B are therefore incorrect. Indeed, such an order can extend beyond the locality where the person is, so answer C is therefore incorrect. Although a RSHO can be made to protect a particular child or a group of children, it extends to children in general (provided they are under 16 years of age) who may be at risk of sexual harm from STEPHENSON.

Crime, para. 1.10.10.24

Answer 8.9

Answer **C** — Section 53 makes it an offence for a person intentionally to control another person's activities relating to prostitution, in any part of the world, where it is done for, or in the expectation of, gain for himself or a third party. Clearly YOUNG is controlling his girlfriend's activity, even although she is happy to go along with it, and it was done with a view to gain, therefore answer B is incorrect. 'Gain' is defined by s. 54 of the Act as any financial advantage, including the discharge of a debt or obligation to pay, or the provision of goods or services (including sexual services) for free, or at a discount. It also covers the goodwill of any person likely to bring such a financial advantage. So this would cover YOUNG inciting his girlfriend to work as a prostitute for DIBLEY, where YOUNG expects this will lead to DIBLEY providing him with cheap drugs at a later date. This future gain therefore makes answer A incorrect. It is immaterial that YOUNG will be in a household with extra income due to his girlfriend's 'activities'; the offence is complete with the goodwill, and answer D is therefore incorrect.

Crime, para. 1.10.11.2

Answer 8.10

Answer **A** — Although the threat was a deception, in that MARKS never intended hurting her husband, rape by deception relates to deception as to the purpose or the person, i.e. the defendant intentionally tells the complainant that digital penetration of her vagina is necessary for medical reasons when in fact it is for his sexual gratification, or where the defendant impersonates the complainant's partner, therefore answer B is incorrect. The violence threatened does not have to be immediate, although the violence or threat must occur either at the time of the relevant act or immediately before it began, therefore answer C is incorrect. Also, s. 75 plainly states that the violence or threat can be against the complainant, or be threats of violence used against a person other than the complainant, therefore answer D is incorrect.

Crime, paras 1.10.3.3, 1.10.3.4

Answer 8.11

Answer **D** — Section 71 of the 2003 Act makes it an offence for a person to engage in sexual activity in a public lavatory. It is not necessary for anyone to have been alarmed or distressed by this activity, therefore answer A is incorrect. This offence can be committed by a male or female against a male or female, which is a change from the old offence of gross indecency, therefore answer B is incorrect. The definition of 'sexual' in s. 71 is idiosyncratic, as s. 71(2) states that 'for the purposes of this section, an activity is sexual if a reasonable person would, in all the circumstances but regardless of any person's purpose, consider it to be sexual'. The difference is that it is unlikely that the third party who witnesses the activity will have information about the purpose of the defendant. For this reason, the sexual activity is limited to that which a reasonable observer would see as unambiguously sexual. This is a wide definition, and includes more than just anal sex; answer C is therefore incorrect.

Crime, para. 1.10.8.3

Answer 8.12

Answer **D** — A person *can* dispute the caution, therefore answers A and B are incorrect. He or she must apply to the court within 14 days of the caution, therefore answer C is incorrect.

Crime, para. 1.10.11.4

Answer 8.13

Answer **B** — Sections 80 to 92 of the Sexual Offences Act 2003 re-enact, with amendments, Part 1 of the Sex Offenders Act 1997, which established a requirement on sex offenders to notify certain personal details to the police. This process is commonly known as 'registration', often referred to loosely as creating a 'sex offenders register'.

Section 84 sets out the requirements on a relevant offender to notify the police of changes to notified details. Under s. 84(1)(c), an offender must notify the police within 3 days, of the address of any premises he has stayed at within the UK, besides his home address, for a 'qualifying period'. This place might be a friend's or relative's house, or a hotel where he has stayed. A qualifying period is defined s. 84(6) as a period of 7 days, or 2 or more periods, in any 12 months, which taken together amount to 7 days. It is an accumulative period of 7 days, not 7 days straight, therefore answer A is incorrect; and for the same reason answer D is incorrect. It is not so exacting as to expect any change of address to be notified, therefore answer C is incorrect.

Crime, para. 1.10.10.5

Answer 8.14

Answer **A** — To prove the offence of kerb-crawling you have to show that the person solicited a woman either persistently, or in circumstances likely to cause annoyance. Although it can be committed from a motor vehicle, it must meet either of the two tests mentioned, so answer B is incorrect. On the subject of persistent soliciting, the prosecution must prove more than one act, i.e. separate approaches to more than one person, or two invitations to the same person. In essence, there must be a degree of repetition.

We now need to examine annoyance; it is sufficient if there was a likelihood of nuisance to other persons in the neighbourhood. BAKER's intention is of no consequence; answer D is therefore incorrect. In determining that likelihood, the character of the area is taken into account, e.g. how common is its use by prostitutes and its residential nature (*Paul* v *DPP* (1989) 90 Cr App R 173). Answer C is incorrect in that, even though the woman propositioned wasn't insulted, other people might have been; given that it is a residential area, this is more than likely. Ask yourself this: would the woman, or any other person in the area, have been annoyed had they known BAKER'S motives?

Crime, para. 1.10.11.4

Answer 8.15

Answer **D** — Section 48 makes it an offence for a person intentionally to cause or incite a child under 18 into prostitution or involvement in pornography in any part of the world. The prostitution or pornography itself does not need to take place for the offence to be committed. This offence is targeted at the recruitment into prostitution or pornography of a child who is not engaged in that activity at the time. The offence would be committed where a 'pimp' makes a living from the prostitution of others and encourages new recruits to work for him. It could also cover the situation where the defendant forces the victim to take part in child pornography for any reason.

Unlike the equivalent adult offence at s. 52, there is no requirement that the prostitution or pornography must be done for the gain of any of the persons involved, therefore KAREN'S mother is as culpable as the others. All 3 persons have incited the child, therefore answers A and B and C are incorrect.

Crime, para. 1.10.5.11

Answer 8.16

Answer **A** — There are two offences here. The first offence is under the Protection of Children Act 1978, of taking, making, distributing, showing, publishing, advertising and possessing with intent to distribute indecent photographs.

The second offence is committed under the Criminal Justice Act 1988, which added the offence of mere possession of such photography.

Therefore, offences would be committed in this scenario by the person distributing, PORTER, and the people possessing, both PORTER and WILLIS (answer B is incorrect).

The offence of distribution is to 'another person'; there is no requirement to distribute to more than one person (answer C is incorrect).

Distributing *will* include lending, which is why answer D is incorrect.

Crime, para. 1.10.5.8

Answer 8.17

Answer **A** — Section 39 makes it an offence for a care worker intentionally to cause or incite another person to engage in sexual activity when that person has a mental disorder and he is involved in his care. It will cover a range of behaviour, including the care worker causing or inciting the victim to have sexual intercourse with him, or causing or inciting the victim to masturbate a third person. The offence is committed if incitement takes place, even if sexual activity does not actually happen because, for example, a relative of the victim intervenes to prevent it. The Act goes on to define what is meant by 'care worker'; it is defined broadly to cover circumstances where a relationship exists because one person has a mental disorder and another person is regularly involved (or likely to be involved) face-to-face in their care, and that care arises from the mental disorder, whether on a primary or ancillary level, and whether on a paid or voluntary basis. It can include, for example, not only doctors, nurses and social workers, but also receptionists, cleaning staff, advocates or voluntary helpers. PAVETT *is* a care worker, therefore answers B and C are incorrect. Section 42(3) states *inter alia* that if the man is a patient for whom services are provided by a National Health Service body then he is included in this offence. The fact he is an outpatient is irrelevant; therefore answer D is incorrect.

Crime, para. 1.10.7.5

Answer 8.18

Answer **A** — There are two relevant offences where a person is premeditating a sexual offence. So what offence is intended? COLLINS clearly intends (although he may not realise it) to commit rape. Under the 2003 Act, rape differs from the offence in the Sexual Offences Act 1956, in that it requires that the defendant does not have a 'reasonable belief' in consent, rather than that he does not have an 'honest belief' in consent. COLLINS' belief is not reasonable, so he will commit rape; answer C is therefore incorrect.

There are two preparatory offences to consider: trespass with intent to commit sexual offence (s. 63); and committing an offence with intent to commit a sexual offence (s. 62). For an offence under s. 63, the person must be 'on any premises where he is a trespasser'. Whilst COLLINS is outside the bedroom window he is not a trespasser; answer B is therefore incorrect. When he breaks the window he has committed a criminal offence, and with the required intent an offence (s. 62) is committed regardless of whether or not the substantive sexual offence is committed; answer D is therefore incorrect.

Crime, paras 1.10.9.1, 1.10.9.2

Answer 8.19

Answer **D** — Section 15 makes it an offence for a person aged 18 or over to meet intentionally, or to travel with the intention of meeting, a child aged under 16 in any part of the world, if he has met or communicated with that child on at least 2 earlier occasions, and intends to commit a 'relevant offence' against that child either at the time of the meeting, or on a subsequent occasion. An offence is not committed if he reasonably believes the child to be 16 or over. The stumbling block to the offence in this question is the lack of a previous meeting. Had there been such previous meeting or communication then the offence would be complete as soon as WISE started travelling towards the meeting, and again when he actually does meet BEN. Note that simply arranging a meeting would not be captured by this offence; answer A is therefore incorrect. Because of the lack of two earlier communications, answers B and

C are incorrect. The section is intended to cover situations where an adult establishes contact with a child through, for example, meetings, telephone conversations or communications on the Internet, and gains the child's trust and confidence so that he can arrange to meet the child for the purpose of committing a 'relevant offence' against the child ('relevant offences' are offences under Part 1 of this Act). The course of conduct prior to the meeting that triggers the offence may have an explicitly sexual content, such as entering into conversations with the child about the sexual acts he wants to engage in when they meet, or sending images of adult pornography. However, the prior meetings or communication need not have an explicitly sexual content and could, for example, simply involve giving the child swimming lessons or selling him sweets.

Crime, para. 1.10.5.4

Answer 8.20

Answer **B** — This offence mirrors that under s. 12 of causing a child to watch a sexual act, with the addition of the perpetrator being in a position of trust. There is a significant difference, however, in that for the abuse of position of trust offences, the child may be 16 or 17 (under 16 for the s. 12 offence); therefore answer C is incorrect. A position of trust is defined by s. 21 of the Act, and in relation to someone in education subsection (5) states:

> This subsection applies if A looks after persons under 18 who are receiving education at an educational institution and B is receiving, and A is not receiving, education at that institution.

'Receiving education at an educational institution' is defined by s. 22(4)(a) as:

> . . . he is registered or otherwise enrolled as a pupil or student at the institution.

'Looks after persons under 18' is a wide caveat, which extends this section beyond the actual teacher/pupil relationship within a specific lesson; therefore answer A is incorrect.

Lastly, s. 12 outlines that it is an offence for a person aged 18 or over intentionally to cause a child, for the purposes of his own sexual gratification, to watch a third person engaging in sexual activity, or to look at an image of a person engaging in a sexual act. The act can be live or recorded, and there is no need for the child to be in close physical proximity to the sexual act. An example would be where he sends a child indecent images over the Internet. In order for an offence to be committed, the adult must act for his own sexual gratification. This ensures that adults showing children sex education material, either in a school or in another setting, will not be liable for this offence. However, this will not be an excuse if the act was done purely for sexual gratification. The term 'image' means a moving or still image, and includes an image produced by any means and, where the context permits, a three-dimensional image; therefore answer D is incorrect.

Crime, para. 1.10.5.5

Answer 8.21

Answer **D** — Section 46 states that where a constable has reasonable cause to believe that a child would otherwise be likely to suffer significant harm, he or she may remove that child to suitable accommodation and keep him or her there.

Answer A is incorrect, as the section allows only a constable to remove the child (known as police protection). There is no requirement for the officer to be in uniform (answer B is therefore incorrect).

The section does not specify that the child should only be taken to a police station or hospital (although these may be suitable places); the child may be taken to any suitable accommodation (which is why C is incorrect).

Crime, para. 1.10.6.7

Answer 8.22

Answer **B** — Voyeurism in certain circumstances is now an offence. Section 67 of the 2003 Act has three subsections outlining what constitutes the offence of voyeurism. Section 67(2) makes it an offence to operate equipment with the intention of enabling another person, for their sexual gratification, to observe a third person doing a private act in the knowledge that the third person has not consented to this being done for another person's sexual gratification. A private act is defined in s. 68 as:

> an act done in a place and in circumstances where the person would reasonably expect privacy and either the person's genitals, buttocks or breasts are exposed or covered only by underwear, or the person is using a lavatory or the person is doing a sexual act that is not of a kind ordinarily done in public.

So it is the fact that the women are involved in a private act that is important in this subsection, and that they did not consent to this being done for another person's sexual gratification that makes the offence, not that they were unaware of the webcam; therefore answer A is incorrect. (Compare to s. 67(1), where the person does not consent to being observed.) It is unimportant that the person who operates the equipment watches the broadcast, or is sexually gratified by it, provided the act is done for another's sexual gratification; answers C and D are therefore incorrect.

Crime, para. 1.10.8.2

Answer 8.23

Answer **A** — Section 87 of the Sexual Offences Act 2003 deals with the method of notification and related matters. It states:

(1) A person gives a notification under section 83(1), 84(1) or 85(1) by —
    (a) attending at such police station in his local police area as the Secretary of State may by regulations prescribe or, if there is more than one, at any of them, and
    (b) giving an oral notification to any police officer, or to any person authorised for the purpose by the officer in charge of the station.

The person must attend within the period of 3 days beginning with any change of his home address. The only option is personal attendance; answers B, C and D are therefore incorrect.

Crime, para. 1.10.10.8

Answer 8.24

Answer **D** — A Sexual Offences Prevention Order:

(a) prohibits the defendant from doing anything described in the order, and
(b) has effect for a fixed period (not less than 5 years) specified in the order or until further order (Sexual Offences Act 2003, s. 107(1)).

Such an order can cover any activity by the offender at all, whether that activity amounts to a criminal offence or a civil wrong, provided it is shown necessary for the purpose of protecting the public, or any particular members of the public, from serious sexual harm from the defendant. As it includes civil wrongs, answer A is incorrect.

A chief officer of police may by complaint to a magistrates' court apply for an order under this section in respect of a person who resides in his police area, or who the chief officer believes is in, or is intending to come to, his police area, if it appears to the chief officer that the person is a qualifying offender. A 'qualifying offender' is defined in s. 106(6) as a person who:

(a) has been convicted of an offence listed in Schedule 3 (other than at paragraph 60) or in Schedule 5,

(b) has been found not guilty of such an offence by reason of insanity,

(c) has been found to be under a disability and to have done the act charged against him in respect of such an offence, or

(d) in England and Wales or Northern Ireland, has been cautioned in respect of such an offence.

So the person does have to have previous convictions; therefore answers B and C are incorrect.

Crime, para. 1.10.10.16

Answer 8.25

Answer **C** — An offender who fails to comply with notification requirements, under s. 91 of the Sexual Offences Act 2003, commits an offence that is triable either way and carries a 5-year tariff on indictment. It is an arrestable offence; answers A, B and D are incorrect.

Crime, para. 1.10.10.17

9 | Child Abduction and Cruelty

STUDY PREPARATION

It is important that officers recognise the significance of some victims — children and other vulnerable groups such as those suffering from a mental disability. Operational officers deal with situations involving these persons on a daily basis; it is important to recognise your powers.

Make sure you know the differences between the two offences under the Child Abduction Act 1984 (person connected and not connected to a child). The emotive issue of child cruelty is also covered here.

QUESTIONS

Question 9.1

JUAN was born in Spain but lives in the UK. He is separated from his wife, GAIL, and their four-year-old son, DAVID. GAIL had custody of DAVID and had refused to let JUAN take DAVID to see his grandparents in Spain. JUAN arranged for his brother to pick up DAVID from school one Friday and take him to Spain. He intended meeting them there, when he finished work later that evening. He knew GAIL would not consent, but intended to return DAVID at the end of the weekend.

In relation to offences that might have been committed under the Child Abduction Act 1984, which of the following is correct?

A Only JUAN is guilty of an offence; his brother is not 'connected with the child'.

B Only JUAN's brother is guilty of an offence; he physically took DAVID out of the UK.

C Both JUAN and his brother are guilty of offences in these circumstances.

D Neither person is guilty, as they intended to return DAVID to the UK.

Question 9.2

SHELLEY, aged 18, was a single parent, who had a baby aged 16 months. One winter, the baby developed a severe case of influenza, which resulted in hypothermia. Eventually the baby died. The baby had been ill for some time, and SHELLEY had not taken her to the doctor. SHELLEY was arrested for the offence of child cruelty, when she reported the death to the police.

What would the prosecution have to prove in order to convict SHELLEY of this offence?

A That her actions in denying medical care were wilful.
B That she was reckless in denying medical care to the child.
C That she intended to deny medical care to the child.
D That her denying medical care for the child included a positive act.

Question 9.3

In relation to child abduction, where the person is not connected to the child (s. 2 of the Child Abduction Act 1984), who is the person entitled to lawful control of the child where the mother and father of the child in question were not married to each other at the time of the birth?

A Both mother and father.
B Either mother or father.
C Mother only.
D Mother and any person who reasonably believed he was the father.

Question 9.4

Section 1(2)(b) of the Children and Young Persons act 1933 provides that a person will have neglected a child who dies as a result of suffocation (not being suffocation caused by disease or the presence of any foreign body in the throat or air passages of the infant) whilst in bed with that child under the influence of drink. There are, however, restrictions on age to this offence.

What are those restrictions?

A The child must be under 2 and the person over 16.
B The child must be under 3 and the person over 16.
C The child must be under 3 and the person over 18.
D The child must be under 2 and the person over 18.

Question 9.5

FRANCES, aged 15, agreed to baby-sit her neighbours' two-year-old child, while her neighbours went out for the evening. During the evening, FRANCES's boyfriend rang her and asked if he could see her. FRANCES checked that the child was asleep, then slipped out of the house to meet her boyfriend. She had been gone from the house for about half an hour, when neighbours found the child wandering down the street in his pyjamas. The child was not injured during the incident.

In relation to the Children and Young Persons Act 1933, which of the following is correct?

A FRANCES has committed an offence of child cruelty through her neglect.

B FRANCES has committed an offence of child cruelty as her actions are wilful.

C FRANCES does not commit an offence of child cruelty in these circumstances.

D FRANCES does not commit an offence of child cruelty as the child was not injured.

ANSWERS

Answer 9.1

Answer **C** — There are two offences under the Child Abduction Act 1984 that deal with taking a child under the age of 16.

Under s. 1 of the Act, an offence takes place where a person connected with a child under the age of 16 takes or sends the child out of the UK without the appropriate consent. This offence *may only be committed by a 'connected person'*; who will include the child's parent, father even if the parents are not married, the legal guardian, or a person with a residence order or lawful custody order.

As JUAN's brother does not fall within this group, he cannot commit this offence. However, to take DAVID lawfully out of the UK, JUAN would require the consent of the mother/guardian/person with a residence order or person with custody.

Obviously JUAN did not have consent to take DAVID out of the UK, and even though he did not actually take him, he committed the offence by sending him. Sending can include 'causing', or 'inducing', a child to go with another, which is why answer B is incorrect.

Under s. 2 of the Act, a person commits an offence if, without lawful authority or reasonable excuse, he takes or detains a child under the age of 16 so as to remove him from the lawful control of any person having lawful control of the child; or so as to keep him out of the lawful control of any person entitled to lawful control of the child (which would include GAIL). This offence may be committed by a person *who is not a 'connected person'*, and would be committed by the brother (which is why answer A is incorrect).

There is no requirement for the abduction to be permanent (making answer D incorrect).

Crime, para. 1.11.2

Answer 9.2

Answer **A** — The circumstances in the question may amount to neglect, but the prosecution must prove that this was *wilful* (not reckless or intentional, which is why answers B and C are incorrect). The issue of *mens rea* was addressed in the case of *R v Sheppard* [1981] AC 394. Lord Diplock explained that:

> . . . the jury must be satisfied (1) that the child did in fact need medical aid at the time at which the parent is charged with failing to provide it (the *actus reus*) and (2) either that the

parent was aware at the time that the child's health might be at risk if it were not provided with medical aid, or that the parent's unawareness of this fact was due to his not caring whether the child's health was at risk or not (the *mens rea*).

There may be an element of 'objective recklessness' in the defendant's behaviour. However, the definition requires proof that a person was wilful in his or her actions.

Answer D is incorrect, as the offence can be committed either by an act, *or* by an omission.

Crime, para. 1.11.3

Answer 9.3

Answer **C** — The person entitled to lawful control of the child where the mother and father of the child in question were not married to each other at the time of the birth is the child's mother only (s. 2(2)(b)); answers A and B are therefore incorrect. If you went for D you may have been confused by s. 1(2), the definition of 'a person connected with a child'. The Child Abduction Act 1984, s. 1(2) states:

A person is connected with a child for the purposes of this section if —
(a) he is a parent of the child; or
(b) in the case of a child whose parents were not married to each other at the time of his birth, there are reasonable grounds for believing that he is the father of the child; or
(c) he is a guardian of the child; or
(d) he is a person in whose favour a residence order is in force with respect to the child; or
(e) he has custody of the child.

There is also a defence to a s. 2 offence which also recognises a person who reasonably believed he was the father of the child; but where they were not married, only the mother is the person entitled to lawful control, so answer D is therefore incorrect.

Crime, para. 1.11.2.1

Answer 9.4

Answer **B** — The Children and Young Persons Act 1933, s. 1(2) states:

(b) where it is proved that the death of an infant under three years of age was caused by suffocation (not being suffocation caused by disease or the presence of any foreign body in the throat or air passages of the infant) while the infant was in bed with some other person who has attained the age of sixteen years, that other person shall, if he was, when he went to bed, under the influence of drink, be deemed to have neglected the infant in a manner likely to cause injury to its health.

The child must be under 3 years of age and, like other aspects of this offence; the person must be at least 16 years of age; answers A, C and D are therefore incorrect.

Crime, para. 1.11.3

Answer 9.5

Answer **C** — To be guilty of an offence under the Children and Young Persons Act 1933, s. 1, an accused must have been over the age of 16 at the time of the offence, and must have 'had responsibility' for the child or young person in question. Although s. 1 creates just one offence, it may take a number of different forms. It may take the form of positive abuse (assault, ill-treatment, abandonment or exposure) or of mere neglect, or it may take the form of causing or procuring abuse or neglect. The abuse or neglect in question must be committed 'in a manner likely to cause unnecessary suffering or injury to health', but the offence is essentially a conduct crime rather than a result crime. It need not therefore be shown that any such injury was caused (answer D is therefore incorrect). FRANCES's actions may well have amounted to an offence under the Act, but she is outside the scope of the legislation by virtue of her age; answers A and B are therefore incorrect.

Crime, para. 1.11.3

10 Offences Amounting to Dishonesty, Deception and Fraud

STUDY PREPARATION

To use the police vernacular, many subjects in this chapter are your 'bread and butter' offences. In the *Police Q & As Road Traffic* book, we stress the importance of knowing basic definitions, in order to recognise the more complex offences. The same applies to many dishonesty offences. You simply cannot get away with not knowing the components that make up the definition of theft. Learning this will assist you with robbery, handling, burglary and aggravated burglary. Similarly, the concept of dishonesty is important to understanding — and proving — a number of offences.

Following on from this, you must be able to recognise the difference between the burglary offences under s. 9(1)(a) and s. 9(1)(b) of the Theft Act 1968, and when a person commits the aggravated offence, by having with them certain articles. Learning the definitions of robbery and handling will also be crucial, as well as the offences under s. 12 of the Act (taking and aggravated vehicle-taking).

There are other offences contained in the chapter that you may not come across regularly, such as abstracting electricity and blackmail. Deception offences are also important.

There is often an overlap between the various offences of deception; it is impor-tant to recognise the differences between each one. Practically, police officers are more likely to encounter deception where it arises from people obtaining property and services, as well as making off without payment. However, for completeness it is important to know all the offences, such as fraud, forgery, obtaining pecu-niary advantage and evading liability.

QUESTIONS

Question 10.1

HARDING was in a shop with PERRY, who picked up a CD intending to steal it. PERRY realised he was being watched by SATO, a store detective, and placed the CD in HARDING'S pocket, without HARDING knowing. Before they left the store, HARDING realised what PERRY had done, and was about to put the CD back, but changed his mind and decided to keep it and try to leave without paying. On their way out, SATO stopped them.

Has HARDING committed an offence in these circumstances?

A No, as PERRY was the one who appropriated the property.

B Yes, he has committed the offence of theft in these circumstances.

C No, as he formed the intent to steal after appropriating the property.

D Yes, he has committed the offence of handling in these circumstances.

Question 10.2

PREECE was out walking in a meadow near her home, when she decided to pick a bunch of wild flowers to create a flower display for her dining room.

Which of the following statements is correct in relation to 'property' as defined by s. 4 of the Theft Act 1968?

A The flowers are wild and are therefore not 'property'.

B Only flowers grown commercially are 'property'.

C 'Wild' relates only to mushrooms, not flowers or foliage.

D Wild flowers become property only if picked for some reward.

Question 10.3

HARVEY was walking past a post office, when he saw an elderly woman coming out. HARVEY produced a knife and threatened her, demanding she handed over her handbag. He had no intention of using the knife, but was trying to make the woman hand over her handbag. The woman was not scared and began hitting him with her bag until he eventually ran away.

Has HARVEY committed the offence of robbery in these circumstances?

A No, as the person was not put in fear of violence being used against her.

B Yes, as he intended to put her in fear of violence being used against her.

C No, but he could have committed attempted robbery.

D Yes, as he has committed attempted theft, using violence.

Question 10.4

LEWIS has had a dispute with his neighbour, PLATT. One night LEWIS got home from the pub, having had too much to drink, and found paint had been poured over his car. He was convinced that PLATT was responsible and so forced his way into PLATT'S house. LEWIS intended to beat PLATT up, causing really serious injury; however, he discovered the house was empty.

In relation to the offence of burglary (under s. 9 of the Theft Act 1968), which of the following is correct?

A An offence under s. 9(1)(b) has been committed even though no grievous bodily harm was caused.

B An offence under s. 9(1)(a) has not been committed as no grievous bodily harm was caused.

C An offence under s. 9(1)(a) has been committed even though no grievous bodily harm was caused.

D An offence under s. 9(1)(a) has not been committed as no assault or theft was carried out.

Question 10.5

PAUL and his family sold their house and bought a large camper van, which they kept permanently on a campsite. While they were out, MORRIS, tired from hitchhiking, broke the door lock to sleep inside the van. Having fallen asleep on a bunk bed, MORRIS was woken up by the sound of children. He ran from the van grabbing some cans of food on the way out.

Which of the following is correct in relation to MORRIS?

A He has *not* committed burglary as a camper van is a vehicle, never a 'building'.

B He has committed burglary, under s. 9(1)(b), as a camper van is a 'building' here.

C He has committed burglary, under s. 9(1)(a), as a camper van is a 'building' here.

D He has *not* committed burglary, as the camper van was not occupied when he entered.

Question 10.6

BOURKE is in the rear garden of a large country house. He forces a ground floor window and enters, and when he enters his intention is to steal. As he is looking around for something to steal, he sees a samurai sword on display. The occupiers, who come in through the front door, disturb BOURKE and he picks up the sword to frighten them. BOURKE points the sword at the occupiers and threatens them with violence. Unafraid, the occupiers approach BOURKE, who drops the sword and runs out of the open front door.

At what stage, if at all, does BOURKE commit an offence of aggravated burglary?

A When he enters the house with intention to steal.

B When he picks up the sword with intention to threaten.

C When he points the sword at the occupiers with intention to threaten.

D No offence of aggravated burglary is committed in these circumstances.

Question 10.7

PARSONS asked his colleague JAMES if he could borrow her motor van to take his family on holiday for the weekend to West Wales. JAMES agreed; however, PARSONS had misled JAMES, and actually takes the motor van to a pop festival with some friends. He returns it in good condition at the end of the weekend.

Has PARSONS committed an offence (under s. 12 of the Theft Act 1968) of taking a vehicle without the owner's consent?

A Yes, he obtained JAMES' permission by deception.

B Yes, but only if the journey was further than the agreed destination.

C No, his deception did not negate the consent he obtained.

D Yes, unless he could show he believed JAMES would have consented.

Question 10.8

WEBB and LARTER were in a supermarket car park when they saw a car with the keys in the ignition. They decided to take the vehicle and WEBB got in the driver's seat; LARTER sat in the front passenger seat. While he was reversing out of the parking place, WEBB struck KANG, a shopper who was walking past. Both WEBB and LARTER got out of the car and ran off, leaving KANG behind with a bruised hip.

Has an offence been committed (under s. 12A of the Theft Act 1968) of aggravated vehicle-taking?

A No, the vehicle was not driven on a road.

B Yes, but only by WEBB, the driver.

C Only if it can be shown that the vehicle was driven dangerously.

D Yes, by both WEBB and LARTER.

Question 10.9

HOWELLS was working for a company that was going through financial difficulties, and as a result, he was laid off. One Friday evening, HOWELLS entered the company office through an insecure window. In order to cause financial hardship to the owners, he linked all the computers up to the Internet, intending that they should all stay on for the weekend.

Has HOWELLS committed the offence of abstracting electricity by his actions?
A Yes, the offence is complete in these circumstances.
B Yes, but a charge of burglary would be more appropriate.
C No, because he has not abstracted or diverted electricity.
D No, using a telephone would not amount to using electricity.

Question 10.10

TAYLOR and RUSSELL met one evening to discuss breaking into an electrical warehouse. It was agreed that TAYLOR would break in and hand the goods to RUSSELL outside in his van. They were joined by BIRCH, who agreed to keep the goods in his house for a few weeks, and MURPHY, who owned a second-hand store and would sell the goods. They agreed that the burglary would take place the following night.

Who, if anyone, has committed the offence of handling stolen goods in these circumstances?
A RUSSELL, BIRCH and MURPHY only.
B All four have committed the offence.
C Only BIRCH and MURPHY have committed the offence.
D None of these people has committed the offence.

Question 10.11

Which of the following statements is/are correct in relation to the offence of handling?
1. A person cannot be convicted of handling if the goods were stolen outside England and Wales.
2. Goods obtained by deception and blackmail are included in the definition of handling.
A Statement 1 only.
B Statement 2 only.

C Both statements 1 and 2.

D Neither statement.

Question 10.12

VINCENT applied for a job with a computer company. He falsely stated in his application form that he was proficient in using several computer packages, which were required by the company in the job description that was sent out with the application form. He was later interviewed, but was unsuccessful and did not get the job.

Has VINCENT committed an offence (under s. 16 of the Theft Act 1968) of obtaining a pecuniary advantage in these circumstances?

A Yes, even though he has not profited from his actions.

B No, because he has not made a financial gain.

C No, he has not received the opportunity to earn remuneration.

D Yes, he deceived the company into interviewing him.

Question 10.13

FRENCH and OSBORN went for a meal in their favourite restaurant, where they ate regularly. During the meal they consumed two bottles of wine each. For a laugh, at the end of the meal they both went to the toilet and climbed out of the window. They intended returning the next day to pay for the meal; however, the restaurant owner did not know this and called the police.

Have FRENCH and OSBORN committed an offence (under s. 3 of the Theft Act 1978) of making off without payment?

A Yes, but they would have a defence if they could show that they thought the owner would have consented in the circumstances.

B No, because they have not deceived the owner into thinking they would pay for the meals.

C No, they have not committed the offence in these circumstances as they intended returning to pay.

D Yes, they have committed the offence, regardless of their intention to pay, and would have no defence in the circumstances.

Question 10.14

GOMEZ was at his friend PETERS' flat and he had with him a stolen credit card, which he had recently used to obtain goods by deception. GOMEZ gave the card to PETERS, so that he could use it the next day. GOMEZ had no intention of using the card again.

Which of the following statements is true, in relation to s. 25 of the Theft Act 1968, regarding 'going equipped'?

A An offence has been committed by PETERS only, as GOMEZ did not intend using the card again.

B An offence has been committed by GOMEZ and PETERS in these circumstances.

C No offence has been committed by either PETERS or GOMEZ, as they were both in a dwelling.

D An offence has been committed by GOMEZ; PETERS commits no offence in these circumstances.

Question 10.15

GORDON fancied CLINTON, who worked with him. He asked her out during a Christmas party, but she refused as she was married. The following day, GORDON sent CLINTON an e-mail, stating that, unless she had sex with him, he was going to phone her husband and tell him they were having an affair.

Has GORDON committed the offence of blackmail in these circumstances?

A Yes, if it can be shown that CLINTON was in fear of the consequences.

B No, as GORDON was not seeking to gain or cause loss.

C Yes, as GORDON has made unwarranted demands with menace.

D No, the offence is committed only where a person demands money or other property.

Question 10.16

SCOTT was homeless and was sitting on a bench in the centre of his local town. He was sitting next to a bucket which had 'SAVE THE CHILDREN' written on it. Believing he was collecting money for charity, several people placed money in the bucket. SCOTT, who was trying to get money for food and not for charity, did not say anything at any time.

Has SCOTT committed an offence (under s. 15 of the Theft Act 1968) of obtaining property by deception?

A No, it cannot be shown that he used words to obtain property by deception.

B Yes, but only if it can be proved that he intended people to be deceived.

C Yes, but only if it can be shown that he was reckless as to whether people were deceived.

D No, he did not use any words or actions to obtain property by deception.

Question 10.17

GRANT is a member of a gym to which she took DUNCAN. At the gym there was a new person working in reception. GRANT showed her membership card to the receptionist, saying, 'She's a member, too, but she forgot her card'. DUNCAN was not a member, but said nothing and was allowed entry, without paying the usual fee for guests.

Who, if anyone, has committed an offence (under s. 1 of the Theft Act 1978) of obtaining a service by deception?

A Both have committed the offence in these circumstances.

B DUNCAN only; there is no offence of obtaining a service for another.

C Neither; the offence applies to a service that will be paid for in the future.

D Neither; they have committed the offence of evasion of liability under s. 2(1)(c) of the Theft Act.

Question 10.18

GORDON ordered some furniture from a second-hand shop. He paid a deposit and was due to pay the remainder on delivery. When the furniture arrived, GORDON gave the delivery driver a cheque, aware that it would not be honoured by the bank. However, he knew that he would have money in the relevant account in a month's time, and would be able to pay the bill then.

Has GORDON committed an offence (under s. 2(1)(b) of the Theft Act 1978) of evasion of liability by deception?

A Yes, but only if the shop owner decides to forgo the payment.

B No, as he does not intend to make a permanent default on the payment.

C Yes, he has made the shop owner wait for the money, which is an offence.

D No, the cheque represents payment, even if later it is not honoured.

Question 10.19

In relation to the intent required for an offence (under s. 17 of the Theft Act 1968) of false accounting, which of the following statements is correct?

1. The defendant's actions must be accompanied by an intention to permanently deprive.

2. The defendant's actions must take place with a view to gain for him and to cause loss to another.

A Both statements.
B Statement 1 only.
C Neither statement.
D Statement 2 only.

Question 10.20

CHANDLER is highly skilled in the forgery field, and produced a sophisticated set of plates from which he made a forged £20 note. Using a high specification laser copier, he photocopied a large quantity of these notes. Before releasing the notes, he spent some in local shops to test their quality.

Which elements of 'false instrument' would CHANDLER be guilty of in these circumstances?

A Making and using a false instrument.
B Copying and making a false instrument.
C Using a false instrument only.
D He is not guilty of any false instrument offence.

Question 10.21

GRAINGER is standing by a bus stop when his friend CARTER arrives in a motor vehicle and offers him a lift. Whilst the vehicle was stationary and switched off, GRAINGER notices that the ignition barrel of the vehicle has been damaged and suspects that the vehicle has been stolen. GRAINGER asks CARTER if the vehicle is stolen and CARTER says, 'What do you think?'. GRAINGER is still unsure whether the vehicle is stolen or not. CARTER goes to start the engine, but police officers arrive and arrest both GRAINGER and CARTER as the vehicle was taken without consent, although this was not by CARTER.

Has GRAINGER committed the offence under the Theft Act 1968, s. 12(1), of allowing himself to be carried?

A Yes, the fact he suspects the car to be stolen and his presence in it is enough — movement of the car is irrelevant.
B Yes, as the vehicle was actually taken without consent and GRAINGER suspects it was.
C No, as the vehicle did not actually move he cannot commit this offence — movement is essential.
D No, mere suspicion is not enough, GRAINGER must know the car is stolen — movement of the car is irrelevant.

Question 10.22

MILLIGAN commits a robbery and steals a mobile phone. He gives it to COMMONS, who works for a mobile telephone company, who alters the unique device identifier and sells the phone on to an unsuspecting buyer.

Considering the Mobile Telephones (Re-Programming) Act 2002, which of the following is true?

A This is an offence from the moment the phone is altered; there is no defence.

B This is an offence from the moment the phone is sold; there is no defence.

C This is an offence from the moment the phone is altered; there is a statutory defence however.

D This is an offence from the moment the phone is sold; there is a statutory defence however.

Question 10.23

KAPARSKI applies for a mortgage from a leading building society, who provide a free mortgage service. He falsely claims that he has a job and that he earns £20,000 per year. He provides accounts and testimonials, which are false, to obtain the mortgage. KAPARSKI hopes to be able to pay the monthly repayments, but this is unlikely given his unemployed status. The building society gives him the loan; however, they would not have done so if it had not been for his practised deception.

Which of the following is correct?

A KAPARSKI has obtained property by deception, as he deceived the building society.

B KAPARSKI has not committed any deception offence, there is no intention to permanently deprive.

C KAPARSKI has not obtained services by deception, as the mortgage service is provided free.

D KAPARSKI has committed an offence of obtaining services by deception.

Question 10.24

FRAMPTON visits his doctor in absolute agony due to a back injury. He demands an injection of a new wonder pain-killing drug, but as it is very expensive his doctor refuses and prescribes a strong pain-killer instead. Infuriated, FRAMPTON pulls a knife from his pocket and threatens to kill the doctor unless he gets the new drug; in fear for his life, the doctor gives him the injection. FRAMPTON apologises for his behaviour and leaves.

110

With respect to blackmail, which of the following is true.

A The offence is complete when the doctor gives FRAMPTON the injection.

B The offence is complete when FRAMPTON threatens the doctor.

C This is not blackmail as FRAMPTON has had no 'gain'.

D This is not blackmail as the doctor has had no loss, the drug belonging to the NHS.

Question 10.25

DIBLEY was employed by a company which had a charge account with a local service station for the purchase of petrol. DIBLEY was a regular visitor and was well known to HASTINGS, who worked as the petrol attendant. Due to staff restructuring DIBLEY was made redundant, and was no longer an employee of the company. DIBLEY is short of fuel and goes to the garage, where he fills the car with petrol. HASTINGS is the attendant and recognises DIBLEY; when told by DIBLEY to charge the petrol to the company's account, he does so.

In relation to obtaining property by deception, which of the following is correct?

A The offence is complete; he has operated a deception on the garage.

B The offence is complete; he has operated a deception on his former employers.

C The offence is not complete; the goods were obtained prior to the operated deception.

D The offence is not complete; the attendant was not deceived as to the identity of the driver.

Question 10.26

DUKE was alleged to have attempted to obtain goods by deception using a credit card. She stated that the card she used belonged to someone she worked with. She claimed that the owner of the card had offered her the use of it and DUKE had signed the card, using her friend's name. She claimed that she did not know that what she was doing was against the law.

In relation to DUKE's actions, which of the following is true?

A DUKE would be viewed as dishonest if a reasonable person believed she was.

B DUKE's knowledge of the law is irrelevant to dishonesty.

C DUKE is not dishonest as she has an honest belief that what she was doing was not illegal.

D DUKE is not dishonest as she had her friend's permission to use the card.

ANSWERS

Answer 10.1

Answer **B** — A person commits theft if he or she dishonestly appropriates property belonging to another with the intention of permanently depriving the other of it (s. 1 of the Theft Act 1968).

Both people have 'appropriated' property in these circumstances, even though HARDING did so after he realised the property was in his pocket (therefore answer A is incorrect). Under s. 3(1), if having come by property (innocently or not) a person later assumes the rights of the owner, he or she commits theft (which is why answer C is incorrect). It is of no relevance that HARDING initially decided to return the property.

As the offence of handling will not be committed during the course of a theft, answer D is incorrect.

Crime, para. 1.12.2.3

Answer 10.2

Answer **D** — Under s. 4(3) of the Theft Act 1968, a person who picks mushrooms growing wild on any land, or who picks flowers, fruit or foliage from a plant growing wild on any land, does not (although not in possession of the land) steal what he or she picks, *unless he or she does it for reward, or for sale or other commercial purpose*. For the purposes of this subsection, 'mushroom' includes any fungus, and 'plant' includes any shrub or tree. Consequently, answers A, B and C are incorrect.

Crime, para. 1.12.2.4

Answer 10.3

Answer **C** — To commit robbery, a person must steal and, immediately before or at the time of doing so and in order to do so, use force on any person, or put *or seek to put* a person in fear of being subjected to force then and there.

Answer B is incorrect, as HARVEY did not steal anything; therefore, he has not committed the full offence of robbery. He would be guilty of attempted robbery in these circumstances, as he sought to put the person in fear of being subjected to force (even though she was not actually scared — making answer A wrong). Further, whether or not he intended to use force is not relevant; his intent that the person should fear that he would is what counts in these circumstances. Lastly, the full offence of theft *must* take place. Therefore, answer D is incorrect.

Crime, para. 1.12.3

Answer 10.4

Answer **C** — A person who enters a building as a trespasser *with intent to inflict* grievous bodily harm commits an offence under s. 9(1)(a) of the Theft Act 1968 (therefore answer B is incorrect). In proving an intention to commit grievous bodily harm under s. 9(1)(a), it is not necessary to prove that an assault was actually committed (*Metropolitan Police Commissioner* v *Wilson* [1984] AC 242) and thus answer D is incorrect.

An offence was not committed under s. 9(1)(b), as a person must be shown to have inflicted grievous bodily harm under that section (answer A is therefore incorrect).

Crime, para. 1.12.4

Answer 10.5

Answer **B** — Something will qualify as a 'building' if it has some degree of permanence. In *B and S* v *Leathley* [1979] Crim LR 314, the Crown Court held that the defendants had committed burglary. They had stolen some meat from a freezer container in a farmyard, which was considered to be permanently in place.

The meaning of 'building' is extended by s. 9(3), and includes an inhabited vehicle or vessel, and applies to any such vehicle or vessel at times when the person having a habitation in it is *not in residence as well as at times when he or she is*. (This makes both answers A and D incorrect.)

Answer C is incorrect because of the intention of the person when he entered the building. MORRIS entered intending to sleep (not one of the prerequisites of s. 9(1)(a)). MORRIS did, however, steal property, having entered as a trespasser, which makes him guilty of burglary under s. 9(1)(b).

Crime, para. 1.12.4.2

Answer 10.6

Answer **D** — Aggravated burglary is defined at s. 10 of the 1968 Act as follows:

A person is guilty of aggravated burglary if he commits any burglary and at the time has with him any firearm or imitation firearm, any weapon of offence, or any explosive.

So, taking it logically, you must establish that the accused had any of the articles listed at the time he committed burglary, contrary either to s. 9(1)(a) or s. 9(1)(b). Certainly burglary is committed at the time BOURKE entered with the requisite intent, but he had no weapons, therefore answer A is incorrect.

If the burglary is under s. 9(1)(b), the offender must have one of the above articles with him when he commits the theft or grievous bodily warm. It is at that point in time that aggravated burglary is committed (and not at the time of entry). *R* v *O'Leary* (1986) 82 Cr App R 341. BOURKE commits no theft, as he leaves the sword behind him, and although an assault has probably taken place by threatening the occupiers with a sword, the injuries do not amount to grievous bodily warm; therefore answers B and C are incorrect. BOURKE has committed many offences in the scenario, but aggravated burglary is not one of them.

Crime, para. 1.12.5

Answer 10.7

Answer **C** — An offence under s. 12 is committed by a person who takes a vehicle without the owner's consent or other lawful authority, for his own or another's use.

The issue of consent was dealt with in the case of *R* v *Peart* [1970] 2 QB 672. The defendant was convicted of the offence, after he falsely represented to the owner of a car that he needed it to drive from Bedlington to Alnwick to sign a contract. The owner let him have the vehicle, provided he returned it that day. As he had intended all along, Peart drove the car instead to Burnley in the evening.

The Court of Appeal subsequently quashed Peart's conviction, by following the decision in *Whittaker* v *Campbell* [1984] QB 318, where it was held that *there is no general principle of law that fraud vitiates consent.*

Consequently, even if consent is obtained by fraud, it is still consent (making answer A incorrect). The case of *Peart* shows that even though the journey taken was different from the one agreed, an offence is still not committed (making answer B incorrect).

Lastly, the defence provided under s. 12(6) would apply *where an offence has been committed*. Since an offence has not been committed in these circumstances, the defence would not apply (which is why answer D is incorrect).

Crime, para. 1.12.7

Answer 10.8

Answer **D** — First, a person must commit an offence under s. 12(1) of the Theft Act 1968 either by taking the vehicle, *or* by being carried in it. Then, under s. 12A, it must be proved that at any time after the vehicle was taken (whether by him or another) and before it was recovered:

- it was driven dangerously on a road or public place; *or*
- owing to the driving of the vehicle, an accident occurred whereby injury was caused to any person; *or*
- owing to the driving of the vehicle, an accident occurred whereby damage was caused to any property other than the vehicle; *or*
- damage was caused to the vehicle.

The Act does not specify that the accident involving an injury to a person should occur on a road (making answer A incorrect).

All that the prosecution has to prove is that *one* of the circumstances above occurred before the car was recovered (*Dawes* v *DPP* (1995) 1 Cr App R 65) (answer C is incorrect for this reason).

Answer A is incorrect because the offence may be committed by either the driver or the passenger, provided one of the circumstances apply.

Crime, paras 1.12.7, 1.12.8

Answer 10.9

Answer **A** — Under s. 13 of the Theft Act 1968, a person who dishonestly uses, without due authority, or dishonestly causes to be *wasted or diverted*, any electricity, shall be guilty of an offence.

As electricity is not 'property', a specific offence was created to deal with its dishonest use or waste. For this reason electricity cannot be 'stolen', and therefore its dishonest use or wastage cannot form an element of burglary (making answer B incorrect).

Diverting a domestic electrical supply so as to bypass the meter, or using another's telephone without authority (*Low* v *Blease* [1975] Crim LR 513) would be examples of this offence, as would unauthorised surfing on the Internet by an employee at work, provided in each case that dishonesty was present (making answers C and D incorrect).

Crime, para. 1.12.10

Answer 10.10

Answer **D** — Quite simply, there can be no offence under s. 22 of the Theft Act 1968, unless goods have been stolen (answers A and B are therefore incorrect). Even though two of the participants have arranged to receive stolen goods, they will not commit the offence until the burglary takes place (answer C is therefore also incorrect).

If the plan ever does come to fruition, TAYLOR, as the person stealing the goods, would not commit the offence. It is debatable whether RUSSELL would do so, if he assisted with the burglary, as he might be guilty of that offence.

Crime, para. 1.12.11

Answer 10.11

Answer **B** — A person *can* be convicted of handling if the goods were stolen outside England and Wales, *but* only if the goods were taken in circumstances which amounted to an offence in the other country (answers A and C are therefore incorrect).

Goods obtained by deception and blackmail *are* included in the definition of handling, which makes statement 2 correct and answer D incorrect.

Crime, para. 1.12.11.1

Answer 10.12

Answer **C** — A person who by any deception dishonestly obtains for himself any pecuniary advantage commits an offence. A pecuniary advantage may be obtained when trying to borrow from an overdraft, taking out a policy of insurance, or when given the opportunity to earn remuneration or greater remuneration in employment (or betting).

In the circumstances given, VINCENT has not obtained the opportunity to earn remuneration, as he was not been given the job. (Although an attempt to commit the offence may be present, answer D is therefore incorrect.)

There is no requirement for a person to actually profit from his or her deception; therefore, if he had been successful with his application, answer A would have been correct. Answer B is incorrect in any circumstances.

Crime, para. 1.13.3

Answer 10.13

Answer **C** — This is a typical question where police officers would think practically and decide, 'I would arrest those'. Avoid this approach and answer questions purely as points of law.

A person commits an offence under s. 3 of the Theft Act 1978 if, knowing that payment on the spot for goods supplied or services received is required, he or she dishonestly makes off without paying *with intent to avoid payment*.

In the scenario, even though the couple have made off without paying, there is no offence if they intend to defer payment to a later date (even though morally their actions may be regarded as wrong!) (Answer D is therefore incorrect).

There is no requirement that the person practised some deception to prove the offence; simply making off with the required intent is enough (which is why answer B is incorrect).

The defence in answer A has been made up and does not exist.

Crime, para. 1.12.15

Answer 10.14

Answer **D** — A person commits an offence under s. 25 of the Theft Act 1968 when, not at his place of abode, he has with him any article for use in the course of or in connection with any burglary, theft or cheat (cheat includes deception).

The offence is designed as a preventative measure and therefore cannot be committed by a deed done in the past. The offence will be committed by a person who has an article with him or her for use by *someone else* (*R v Ellames* [1974] 3 All ER 130).

Applying the Act to this scenario, GOMEZ was not at his place of abode and had with him a credit card, which he intended PETERS to use in the future in a cheat (offence committed, even though he had no intention of using it again, which is why answer A is incorrect).

The card was given to PETERS and, although he intended using it, he *was* at his place of abode. Consequently, no offence is committed until PETERS leaves his house, and therefore answer B is incorrect.

Answer C is incorrect because the offence may be committed by a person in a dwelling — provided it is not the place where he or she lives!

Crime, para. 1.12.14

Answer 10.15

Answer **B** — Blackmail is committed when a person, with a view to gain for himself or another, or with intent to cause loss to another, makes any unwarranted demands with menaces (s. 21 of the Theft Act 1968).

Under s. 34 of the Act, 'gain' and 'loss' mean to gain or lose in money or other property. It will not apply where a person is making demands for sexual favours. Consequently, answers A, C and D are incorrect.

Crime, para. 1.12.16

Answer 10.16

Answer **C** — The prosecution would have to show that SCOTT either intended people to believe he was collecting money for charity, *or* that he was reckless to that fact (making B incorrect). The reckless element is subjective, although the prosecution would have to show that the defendant at least gave some thought to his conduct (*R* v *Goldman* [1997] Crim LR 894).

Conduct can include *omissions* (*R* v *Shama* [1990] 1 WLR 661); therefore, the fact that the person did not say or do anything would not provide a defence (which is why answers A and D are incorrect).

Crime, para. 1.13.2

Answer 10.17

Answer **A** — A deception occurs where a person has induced another to confer a benefit by doing some act, or causing or permitting some act to be done, on the understanding that a benefit *has been or will* be paid for (therefore answer C is incorrect).

The Court of Appeal has accepted that obtaining a service for another will amount to an offence under s. 1 of the Theft Act 1978 (*R* v *Nathan* [1997] Crim LR 835), making answer B incorrect.

Evasion of liability is dealt with later in the chapter, but the circumstances outlined do not constitute an offence under s. 2(1)(c), as there is no provision under the section in respect of obtaining an abatement of liability *for another* (therefore answer D is incorrect).

Crime, para. 1.13.4

Answer 10.18

Answer **B** — A person commits an offence under s. 2(1)(b) of the Theft Act 1978 if, with intent to make *permanent default* in whole or in part on any existing liability to make a payment, or with intent to let another do so, he or she dishonestly induces the creditor or any person claiming payment on behalf of the creditor to wait for payment (whether or not the due date for payment is deferred) or to forgo payment.

Even though he has made the shop owner wait for the money, it would have to be shown that GORDON intended *permanently* to default on the payment (for example, if GORDON changed address after presenting the cheque), which is why answer C is incorrect.

Unlike the other two offences in s. 2(1), it is not necessary under s. 2(1)(b) to show that the person to whom the money was owed decided to forgo all or part of the payment (making answer A incorrect).

Answer D is incorrect because s. 2(3) of the Act states:

For purposes of subsection (1)(b) a person induced to take in payment a cheque or other security for money by way of conditional satisfaction of a pre-existing liability is to be treated *not* as being paid but as being induced to wait for payment.

Crime, para. 1.13.5

Answer 10.19

Answer **C** — Under s. 17 of the Theft Act 1968, a person must act dishonestly with a view to gain for himself or another, *or* (not and) with intent to cause loss to another.

The offence is complete when a person destroys, defaces, conceals or falsifies any account, or any record or document made or required for any accounting purpose; or in furnishing information for any purpose produces or makes use of any account, or any such record or document as aforesaid, which to his knowledge is or may be misleading, false or deceptive in a material particular.

Unlike theft, there is no requirement to prove an intention permanently to deprive, but there is a need to show dishonesty.

Therefore, *both* statements are incorrect and answers A, B and D are consequently incorrect.

Crime, para. 1.13.7.1

Answer 10.20

Answer **D** — Quite simply, offences classed as forgery include virtually every kind of document *except* bank notes. Therefore, as he has been involved in 'forging' bank notes, CHANDLER cannot commit the offences of making and using a false instrument (answer A is incorrect), copying and making a false instrument (answer B is incorrect) and using a false instrument (answer C is incorrect). Offences relating to currency are dealt with by the Forgery and Counterfeiting Act 1981.

Crime, para. 1.13.7.4

Answer 10.21

Answer **C** — On a charge of driving or allowing himself to be carried in or on a conveyance taken without authority, it must be proved that the accused knew that the conveyance had been taken without lawful authority (*R* v *Diggin* (1980) 72 Cr App R 204, *Boldizsar* v *Knight* [1980] Crim LR 653); therefore, answers A and B are incorrect. However, it seems that the accused need not be aware that the taker took the conveyance for his own or another's use.

It is also not enough for the prosecution to prove that the accused was in or on the conveyance. There must have been some movement of the conveyance (*R* v *Miller* [1976] Crim LR 417; also see *Diggin*). If a taker of a motor vehicle offers a person a lift and he gets into the seat next to the driver, the person is not allowing himself to be driven before the driver turns on the ignition switch (*Diggin*).

So answer D is almost correct. However, it is essential that a conveyance be moved in order for it to be taken, however small that movement may be, and this is the same even though the accused is only allowing himself to be carried. Answer D is therefore incorrect.

Crime, para. 1.12.7.3

Answer 10.22

Answer **C** — This offence was created to try to prevent the increasing criminal activity involving mobile handsets. The offence is committed where the unique identifier is either changed or interfered with, and is not reliant on a future sale of the phone; answers B and D are therefore incorrect. There is, however, a statutory defence, exclusive to manufacturers or those with written consent of the manufacturers; answer A is therefore incorrect.

Crime, para. 1.12.11.7

Answer 10.23

Answer **D** — On a charge of obtaining property by deception contrary to the Theft Act 1968, s. 15(1), the prosecution must prove that the accused acted dishonestly and with the intention of permanently depriving another of the property. As to intention permanently to deprive, the whole of the definition of this concept in the Theft Act 1968, s. 6, is applicable to s. 15 by virtue of s. 15(3). In this question, the accused does not have such intention; answer A is therefore incorrect.

The Theft Act 1978, s. 1(2), defines 'services' in terms of benefits (which would include accommodation, travel, education, medical care, etc.), but excludes benefits which are provided gratuitously. In *R v Halai* [1983] Crim LR 624, the Court of Appeal held that a building society had not provided services merely by allowing the accused to open a savings account because building societies do not charge any fees for such accounts. The position would be different if the accused practices his deception in order to open a current account with a bank which charges for services provided to such accounts (*R v Shortland* [1995] Crim LR 893). It was also held in *Halai* that a mortgage advance falls outside the definition of 'services'. This ruling was widely criticised (and seems downright daft), but has been captured by the Theft Act 1978, s. 1(3), which was inserted by the Theft (Amendment) Act 1996, s. 4. This puts the situation of obtaining a loan by deception squarely within the offence of obtaining services; answers B and C are therefore incorrect.

Crime, paras 1.13.2, 1.13.4.1

Answer 10.24

Answer **B** — The points to prove for an offence of blackmail are:

- with a view to gain;
- for self or another; *or*
- with intent to cause loss to another;
- made an unwarranted demand with menaces.

Using a knife to threaten to kill someone is most certainly an unwarranted demand ('unwarranted demand' is defined as an unreasonable or unfair demand) and menacing! 'Menaces' is loosely delineated as threat (including a veiled one) of any action detrimental or unpleasant to the person addressed. And the offence is complete at the time the demand is made, not when its desired consequences are brought about; answer A is therefore incorrect.

As the demand must be made with a view to the person's gain, has FRAMPTON actually 'gained'? The gain must be in money or other property and can be temporary or permanent. In a case not mentioned in the manual, it was held that the drug was property and the injection involved 'gain' to the accused as he achieved pain relief. The fact that it was injected into him rather than being handed over did not mean that FRAMPTON did not gain that property; answer C is incorrect. There does not have to be a loss, provided the demand is made with a view to gain; answer D is therefore incorrect.

Crime, para. 1.12.16

Answer 10.25

Answer **C** — Where a deceit is practised after the goods are obtained, there will be no operating deception, which is a prerequisite for a s. 15 offence. So although DIBLEY has deceived the garage, as the deceit occurred after he obtained the goods, the most appropriate charge would be theft; answer A is thus incorrect. Similar principles are found in the 1978 Act. If, for example, the accused has paid a hotelier with a stolen cheque for services already provided, this cannot in itself amount to an offence under the Theft Act 1978, s. 1, because the services have already been obtained (*R v Collis-Smith* [1971] Crim LR 716). In *R v Coady* [1996] Crim LR 518, where the accused acted in a manner similar to this question, it was held that a deception must operate on the victim (who must be human, therefore answer B is incorrect) before ownership of the property is passed to the offender. In *Coady* the accused's conviction was quashed because the trial judge had failed to warn the jury of the requirement that the deception must have been operating on the attendant before the petrol was obtained. The deception relates to the practice, not the identity, of the defendant; answer D is therefore incorrect.

Crime, para. 1.13.2

Answer 10.26

Answer **B** — The Court of Appeal in *R v Ghosh* [1982] QB 1053 established two principles which apply to dishonesty, now known as the famous *Ghosh* test. This test means the jury determine whether the accused was acting dishonestly in two stages:

[1] . . . a jury must first of all decide whether according to the ordinary standards of reasonable and honest people what was done was dishonest. If it was not dishonest by those standards, that is the end of the matter and the prosecution fails.

If it was dishonest by those standards, then the jury must consider [the second question].

[2] . . . the jury must consider whether the defendant himself must have realised that what he was doing was by [the standards of reasonable and honest people] dishonest.

You have to show more than just the 'reasonable person' view; answer A is therefore incorrect, as the offender must realise the dishonesty of what she was doing. The courts have held that, on the question of dishonesty, the defendant's knowledge of the law, whether criminal or civil law, is irrelevant (*R v Lightfoot* (1992) 97 Cr App R 24); answer C is therefore incorrect. Lastly, permission or not, if a reasonable person believes that the actions were dishonest *and* the accused realises that she was dishonest, the *Ghosh* test will be met; answer D is therefore incorrect.

Crime, para. 1.12.2.2

11 | Criminal Damage

STUDY PREPARATION

The definition of criminal damage needs attention in the first instance, and you will have to know the various components, such as lawful excuse, protection, recklessness, damage, property and belonging to another. In addition to these statutory issues there are many decided cases on each of these points.

It is important to learn the basic definition, before turning to the aggravated offences. Each one of these is similar to the other, with the defendant's intent being of key significance.

It is also worth paying attention to contamination of goods. Although the offences associated with the definition are reasonably long and complicated, this is an area that may receive considerable further attention in the current climate of terrorist threats.

This is the penultimate chapter for you to tackle — you're almost there . . .

QUESTIONS

Question 11.1

PETERS lived in the countryside and was having trouble with a fox, which had attacked her cat. One day she managed to corner the fox in her neighbour's field, but it escaped into a hole. PETERS set fire to the grass surrounding the hole, but unfortunately the fire spread to her neighbour's shed. When the fire was eventually extinguished, they found that the fox had been killed, as well as two of the farmer's chickens and some wild geese that he had tamed some time before.

Given that PETERS may be guilty of reckless criminal damage to property (the shed), would she also be guilty of criminal damage to any of the animals?

A Yes, to the chickens only.

B Yes, to the chickens and the geese.

C No, as animals are not property.

D Yes, to all three animals.

Question 11.2

POWERS and WARNE were in the centre of their local town. It had been snowing and they decided to have a snowball fight. POWERS made a snowball and threw it at WARNE, who ducked. The snowball smashed through a nearby shop window. POWERS was arrested, but says in his interview that he had not realised that any damage would be caused.

What must the arresting officers prove in order to show that he had been reckless?

A That the risk of damage to the window was obvious and POWERS should have seen that risk.

B That the risk of damage to the window would have been obvious to a reasonably intelligent person and that POWERS ignored that risk.

C That the risk of damage to the window would have been obvious to POWERS if he had stopped to think about it.

D That the risk of damage to some property was foreseen by POWERS and he went on to take that risk.

Question 11.3

SINGH worked in a car park. While at work on a very hot day, he was told about a dog that was locked in one of the cars, with the windows closed. SINGH went to the car and saw the dog lying on the back seat. He thought that the dog was suffering and, believing that the owner would have consented, he smashed the window. As he was doing this, the owner of the car, MORGAN, returned. It appeared that the dog had not been there long, and it was asleep. MORGAN accused SINGH of causing criminal damage.

In relation to the defence under s. 5(2)(a) of the Criminal Damage Act 1971 (belief that he had consent to the damage to the property in question) only, which of the following statements is correct?

A SINGH could claim this defence if he could show that a reasonable person would have consented to the damage.

B   SINGH could claim this defence if he believed that MORGAN would have consented, had she known the circumstances.

C   SINGH could *not* claim this defence as he was reckless in these circumstances.

D   SINGH could *not* claim this defence as MORGAN, knowing the circumstances, would not have consented.

Question 11.4

When proving an offence under s. 1(2) of the Criminal Damage Act 1971 (aggravated criminal damage), what *mens rea* must be shown?

A   That the person intended to cause criminal damage and intended to endanger a person's life.

B   That the person intended or was reckless as to whether damage would be caused, and intended or was reckless as to whether life would be endangered.

C   That the person intended or was reckless as to whether a person's life would be endangered.

D   That the person intended to cause criminal damage only, and was reckless as to whether a person's life would be endangered.

Question 11.5

The Anti-social Behaviour Act, s. 54 makes it an offence to sell aerosol paint to whom?

A   Someone who is 16 years of age or under.

B   Someone who is or appears to be 16 years of age or under.

C   Someone who is under 16 years of age.

D   Someone who is or appears to be under 16 years of age.

Question 11.6

When considering an offence under s. 2 of the Criminal Damage Act 1971 (threats to destroy or damage property), what must the prosecution prove?

A   That the accused intended that the victim would fear that the damage would be carried out immediately.

B   That the accused intended to cause damage and intended to induce fear that damage would be carried out.

C   That the accused intended that the victim would fear that the damage would be carried out.

D That the victim did in fact fear that the accused would carry out the threat to cause damage.

Question 11.7

WILKINS and MARTIN are members of an extreme animal rights group. MARTIN applied for a job in a zoo, and they planned that if he was successful, he would damage customers' cars by placing sharp tacks under the tyres. WILKINS bought ten packets of tacks at a DIY store the day before MARTIN's interview, intending to give them to him if he got the job.

Has either person committed an offence under s. 3 of the Criminal Damage Act 1971 (having articles with intent to damage property)?

A Only WILKINS; he has control of the articles, intending that MARTIN should use them to cause damage.

B Neither person, as WILKINS does not intend to use the articles himself to cause criminal damage.

C Both people, because of their joint intent that MARTIN should use the articles to cause damage.

D Neither person, as the intent to commit damage is conditional on MARTIN being successful in his interview.

Question 11.8

THATCHER works in a butcher's shop. As a joke, on 1 April he came in early and sprinkled icing sugar on some meat on display. He then left a note for his boss, claiming to be from an animal rights group, saying they had sprinkled rat poison on the food. Unfortunately, before he was able to stop him, his boss threw the meat away.

Has THATCHER committed an offence under s. 38 of the Public Order Act 1986 (contamination of goods)?

A Yes, because he has caused economic loss to his employer.

B No, because he has not caused public alarm or anxiety.

C No, because he has not actually contaminated any goods.

D No, because he only intended his employer to treat it as a joke.

ANSWERS

Answer 11.1

Answer **B** — Section 10 of the Criminal Damage Act 1971 describes 'property' as:

... property of a tangible nature, whether real or personal, including money and — (a) including wild creatures which have been tamed or are ordinarily kept in captivity ...

Quite simply, the geese have been tamed and are therefore 'property'. Likewise, the chickens are ordinarily kept in captivity and are therefore 'property'. The fox is not 'property', as it is neither tamed, nor ordinarily kept in captivity. Consequently, answers A, C and D are incorrect.

Crime, para. 1.14.2.3

Answer 11.2

Answer **D** — What is important now to the concept of recklessness (since the House of Lords considered it in *R* v *G & R* [2003] 3 WLR 1060) is that the defendant had foreseen the risk yet gone on to take it. Their Lordships held that a person acts recklessly (in a criminal damage case) where:

• With respect to a *circumstance*, he or she is aware of a risk that existed or would exist.
• With respect to a *result or consequence*, he or she is aware of a risk that it would occur and it is, in the circumstances known to him or her, unreasonable to take the risk.

It is more than the risk being obvious to the offender; he or she must then go on to take that risk with such knowledge: answers A and C are therefore incorrect. The previous case law held that a 'reasonable person' test existed for the risk. This has been overturned by *R & G* and the test now sits squarely with the offender's knowledge of the risk, and his or her willingness to take that risk; answer B is therefore incorrect.

Crime, para. 1.14.2.8

Answer 11.3

Answer **B** — A person shall be treated as having lawful excuse under s. 5(2) of the Criminal Damage Act 1971:

(a) if at the time of the act or acts alleged to constitute the offence he believed that the person or persons whom he believed to be entitled to consent to the destruction of or damage to the property in question had so consented, or would have so consented to it if he or they had known of the destruction or damage and its circumstances . . .

Provided a person holds a genuine, reasonably held belief that the owner of the property would have consented had they known the circumstances, he or she will not be guilty of an offence. (It must be based on the defendant's own belief, not that of a reasonable person or the owner of the property, making answers A and D incorrect.)

SINGH is not guilty of recklessness; he intended to break the window (making C incorrect).

Crime, para. 1.14.2.6

Answer 11.4

Answer **B** — A person is guilty of an offence under s. 1(2) of the Criminal Damage Act 1971, if they damage/destroy property intending *or* reckless as to whether damage is caused to their own property, or another's, *and* they intend *or* are reckless as to whether a person's life is endangered.

Either the elements of intent *or* recklessness must be proved in relation to both the damage and the endangerment to life for this offence to be made out. All four answers are fairly similar, but only answer B contains all the elements required to prove the offence. Consequently, answers A, C and D are incorrect.

Please note the change in the concept of recklessness brought about by the decision of the House of Lords in *R* v *G & R* [2003] 3 WLR 1060.

Crime, para. 1.14.3

Answer 11.5

Answer **C** — A person commits the offence by selling the aerosol to a person under 14 years of age. There is a defence courtesy of s. 4, for the person who reasonable believes the person was not under the age of 16 and took all reasonable steps to determine the purchaser's age. The section makes no mention of the apparent age of the purchaser; answers A, C and D are incorrect.

Crime, para. 1.14.7

Answer 11.6

Answer **C** — This is an offence of intention; that is, the key element is the *defendant's intention* that the person receiving the threat fears it would be carried out.

The s. 2 offence under the Criminal Damage Act 1971, which originates from the need to tackle protection racketeers, is very straightforward: there is no need to show that the other person actually feared or even believed that the threat would be carried out (making answer D incorrect).

Also, there is no need to show that the defendant intended to carry out the threat; nor does it matter whether the threat was even capable of being carried out (which is why answer B is incorrect).

Answers A and C are similar; however, C is correct because there is no requirement to show that the accused intended to cause fear of *immediate* damage.

Crime, para. 1.14.5

Answer 11.7

Answer **A** — Section 3 of the Criminal Damage Act 1971 states:

A person who has anything in his custody or under his control, intending without lawful excuse to use it or cause or permit another to use it —
(a) to destroy or damage any property belonging to some other person; or
(b) to destroy or damage his own or the user's property in a way which he knows is likely to endanger the life of some other person;
shall be guilty of an offence.

Answer B is incorrect, as a person may have control of articles which he or she intends to permit another to use. Answer C is incorrect, as MARTIN did not have the articles in his custody or control at any time.

Answer D is incorrect because a conditional intention to use an article if given circumstances arise will amount to an offence (*R v Buckingham* (1976) 63 Cr App R 159).

Crime, para. 1.14.6

Answer 11.8

Answer **D** — Under s. 38 of the Public Order Act 1986, it is necessary to prove that a person contaminated or interfered with goods, or made it appear that goods have been contaminated or interfered with, or threatened or claimed to have done so.

However, the person must have done so *with the intention* of causing public alarm or anxiety, or of causing injury to members of the public consuming or using the goods, or of causing economic loss to any person by reason of the goods being shunned by members of the public, or of causing economic loss to any person by reason of steps taken to avoid such alarm or anxiety, injury or loss.

Therefore, even though THATCHER in the circumstances may have contaminated goods, and even caused economic loss, he did not do so with the required intention and cannot be guilty of this offence. (Answer A is therefore incorrect.)

Had THATCHER been proved to have had the required intent, answers B and C would still be incorrect, because there is no need to prove a person actually caused public alarm/anxiety, and the offence may be committed without actually contaminating goods.

Crime, para. 1.14.8

12 | Offences Against the Administration of Justice and Immigration Offences

STUDY PREPARATION

This chapter tests your knowledge of those offences which exist to deter people from interfering with the proper course of justice. Included in this chapter are questions relating to perjury, false statements and immigration offences. The events of 11 September 2001 prompted swift and significant changes to immigration offences throughout the world. The common law offence of perverting the course of justice is included, as are the statutory offences of intimidating witnesses and jurors. Particular crimes relating to those who assist offenders by protecting or hiding them are tested, as are those relating to wasting police time — an area that may also come into greater use as pressures on police resources intensify. Lastly, contempt of court and corruption bring the chapter, the book and your studies to an end.

Well done!

QUESTIONS

Question 12.1

DAVIDSON is giving evidence in court in his own defence. He is not religious and has taken the affirmation instead of swearing on the Bible. The evidence he gives is that he was not at the scene of the offence, stating he was elsewhere. This is in fact untrue and DAVIDSON knows it.

Has DAVIDSON committed perjury?

A No, perjury cannot be committed by a defendant.

B No, perjury can only be committed by a 'sworn' witness.

C Yes, provided it is shown he intended to mislead the court.

D Yes, he has given false testimony and knows it to be false.

Question 12.2

BOWDITCH has committed an offence which, though not an 'arrestable' offence under s. 24 of the Police and Criminal Evidence Act, nevertheless carries a statutory power of arrest. Constable SOUTHALL is making enquiries into the whereabouts of BOWDITCH and goes to BOWDITCH's sister's house to see if he is there. BOWDITCH is in fact in the house, and his sister knows he is. BOWDITCH has told her that he committed the offence. Constable SOUTHALL asks the sister if she has seen BOWDITCH. She says she hasn't and that he has gone to his cousin's home in Manchester. Having no reason to disbelieve her, the officer leaves, intending to pursue the matter with Greater Manchester Police.

Which of the following statements is true?

A The sister has committed an offence of assisting an offender.

B The sister has committed an offence of harbouring an offender.

C The sister has not committed an offence of assisting an offender.

D The sister has committed no offence.

Question 12.3

BOWDEN is the local authority building works manager. Aware that his girlfriend has just moved into a new, rather dilapidated house, BOWDEN arranges for a team of workers from the council to go to her house and do some work. They use materials that were meant for council premises and they do the work in council time.

Considering corruption offences, which, if any, offence has BOWDEN committed?

A Common law corruption.

B Public bodies corruption.

C Corruption of agents.

D He has not committed any offence of corruption.

Question 12.4

SUTTON makes a mobile telephone call to his neighbour stating that a child has just fallen into the river and been swept downstream. His neighbour calls the police and a search commences. Several officers are involved, and the force air support unit is called in to assist. Later SUTTON admits he made the incident up as he had received a speeding ticket last week. In total 25 police hours were wasted and the cost came to £21,000.

Which of the following statements is true?

A   SUTTON is guilty of wasting police time as the limit of 21 hours has been passed.

B   SUTTON is guilty of wasting police time as he falsely raised fears for the safety of a person.

C   SUTTON is not guilty of wasting police time as he did not contact the police himself.

D   SUTTON is not guilty of wasting police time as the cost did not exceed £25,000.

Question 12.5

KANG is originally from Pakistan, but is now a British citizen. His brother (who is not a British citizen) wishes to come to Britain on a permanent basis, but has falsely filled out an entry application stating he is coming on holiday. KANG has signed this form to say that his brother will stay with him on holiday for two weeks. KANG knows this to be false.

Who, if either, commits an offence under s. 24A of the Immigration Act 1971?

A   KANG only, as a British citizen.

B   Both KANG and his brother.

C   His brother only, as he is not a British citizen.

D   Neither, this offence applies only to applications for citizenship.

Question 12.6

MULLINS has been sold laminate flooring, which is defective, and has issued a county court claim against ACME Co. Ltd, who supplied the goods. CROCKETT is an expert laminate floor fitter and intends to give evidence on MULLIN's behalf at court. In order to prevent this, ACME's managing director have written a letter to CROCKETT warning him that he will lose business if he gives evidence against the company.

Does this letter amount to intimidation of a witness?

A   Yes, provided there was intention to intimidate CROCKETT.

B Yes, provided the company were reckless as to whether CROCKETT would be intimidated.

C No, as the threat was not made in person.

D No, intimidating witnesses applies only to criminal courts cases, not county court cases.

Question 12.7

LANEY is an accredited Police Community Support Officer (PCSO) and is dealing with ARMSTRONG for a fixed penalty offence. He requires ARMSTRONG to provide his name and address. ARMSTRONG refuses and LANEY exercises his power of detention as provided by Sch. 4 to the Police Reform Act 2002. ARMSTRONG is less than impressed at this, and pushes the PCSO over and makes good his escape.

Consider the offence at common law of escaping. Which of the following is correct?

A ARMSTRONG has committed this offence, and is arrestable.

B ARMSTRONG has committed this offence; however, there is no power of arrest.

C ARMSTRONG has not committed this offence, as it relates to escaping from prisons, etc.

D ARMSTRONG has not committed this offence, and it relates to lawful custody, i.e. by a police officer.

Question 12.8

COOK is a potential juror at Crown Court. His wife works behind the bar of the 'Red Lion'. HUGHES, a friend of MAKINGS, who is about to stand trial for murder, enters the 'Red Lion' and approaches COOK's wife. HUGHES says, 'Tell your old man Makings is not guilty, or things could get very nasty for him and you'. HUGHES is intending to influence the jury in the case.

Consider an offence under s. 51 of the Criminal Justice and Public Order Act 1994, intimidation of witnesses and jurors. Which of the following is true?

A No offence; COOK is only a potential juror.

B No offence as only a third party, the wife, was intimidated.

C This is an offence, provided the wife felt threatened or intimidated.

D This is an offence due to HUGHES's intention.

Question 12.9

Constable WESSON is engaged on house to house enquiries following a murder. He interviews a female neighbour of the victim, SMITH, at her house. A short time into her account she breaks down and confesses that she was guilty of the murder. Having ascertained her guilt, he tells her that he will make out a false report if she gives him oral sex, which she does. He then does not tell anybody what he found and files a false report. SMITH is not arrested for 2 months, but is duly imprisoned for the offence.

Has Constable WESSON committed an offence of assisting an offender under s. 4 of the Criminal Law Act 1967?

A   Yes, when he tells SMITH that he will keep quiet about what he knows.

B   Yes, when he submits the false report.

C   No, as she did not escape justice.

D   No, police officers cannot commit this offence.

Question 12.10

It is an offence under s. 36 of the Criminal Justice Act 1925 to make an untrue statement to procure a passport.

In relation to this offence, which of the following is true in relation to the person making that statement?

A   That he makes the statement believing it not to be true.

B   That he makes the statement knowing or believing it not to be true.

C   That he makes the statement and is reckless as to whether it is true or not.

D   That the statement is to his knowledge untrue.

ANSWERS

Answer 12.1

Answer **D** — Section 1(1) of the Perjury Act 1911 states:
If any person lawfully sworn as a witness or as an interpreter in a judicial proceeding wilfully makes a statement material in that proceeding, which he knows to be false or does not believe to be true, he shall be guilty of perjury . . .

'Any person' includes the defendant and therefore answer A is incorrect. There is no requirement to show intention to mislead the court; simply making the statement deliberately is enough, and therefore answer C is incorrect. It is possible for a witness or interpreter to make a solemn affirmation in place of the oath, whether or not the taking of an oath would be contrary to his or her religious beliefs, and s. 15(2) of the Perjury Act 1911 provides that references therein to 'oaths' and 'swearing' embrace affirmations. The affirming witness is therefore equally subject to the Perjury Act 1911 and answer B is also incorrect.

Crime, para. 1.15.2

Answer 12.2

Answer **C** — The offence of assisting offenders applies only where an arrestable offence (as per s. 24 of the Police and Criminal Evidence Act) has been committed, and therefore answer A is incorrect. Harbouring offenders applies to people who have escaped from a prison or other institutions, and therefore answer B is incorrect. The sister has almost certainly committed an offence of perverting the course of public justice and, arguably, wasting police time, under s. 5(2) of the Criminal Law Act 1967; answer D is therefore incorrect.

Crime, paras 1.15.7, 1.15.9

Answer 12.3

Answer **A** — Common law corruption is described in *R* v *Bembridge* (1783) 3 Doug 327: '[a] man accepting an office of trust concerning the public is answerable criminally to the [the Crown] for misbehaviour in his office . . . by whomever and in whatever way the officer is appointed'. In *R* v *Bowden* [1996] 1 WLR 98, the Court of Appeal held that a local authority manager, who improperly arranged for his men to carry out work at his girlfriend's house, was guilty of the offence of common law corruption. Public bodies corruption is defined in the Public Bodies Corrupt Practices Act 1889 as 'every person who shall by himself or by or in conjunction with any other person, corruptly solicit or receive, or agree to receive, for himself, or for any other person, any gift, loan, fee, reward, or advantage', which is not the case here so answer B is incorrect. Corruption of agents is described in the Prevention of Corruption Act 1906 as 'if any agent corruptly accepts or obtains, or agrees to accept or attempts to obtain, from any person, for himself or for any other person, any gift or consideration as an inducement or reward', which again is not the case here, so answer C is incorrect. As an offence has been committed, answer D is incorrect.

Crime, para. 1.15.12

Answer 12.4

Answer **B** — The definition of this offence (Criminal Law Act 1967, s. 5(2)) includes the phrase 'making to any person a false report' and therefore answer C is incorrect. Contrary to popular belief, there is no time limit for this offence, and answer A is also incorrect. Likewise, there is no monetary value placed on this offence and therefore answer D is incorrect.

Crime, para. 1.15.10

Answer 12.5

Answer **C** — Section 24A of the Immigration Act 1971 is aimed at the actions of non-British citizens only, so as a British citizen, KANG can never commit this offence (answers A and B are incorrect). It applies to any application to obtain or seek to obtain leave to enter the UK in any circumstances, including holidays, and therefore answer D is incorrect. KANG'S brother commits the offence as he uses means which include deception to achieve his leave to enter. KANG would, however, still commit offences contrary to the interests of justice.

Crime, para. 1.16.1.4

Answer 12.6

Answer **A** — Section 39 of the Criminal Justice and Police Act 2001 extended the offences of intimidation of witness offences outlined in s. 51 of the Criminal Justice and Public Order Act 1994 to proceedings in civil cases. The 1994 Act applies to the investigation or trial of those in criminal proceedings. Answer D is therefore incorrect. The new offence is very similar to the 1994 Act offence and is an offence of specific intent, so recklessness will not suffice (answer B is therefore incorrect). The offence includes doing any act, provided it was with the intention of intimidating a witness and provided the defendant knew the person might be a witness. This would include writing letters, making phone calls, etc., and is not limited to personal threats (answer C is also incorrect).

Crime, para. 1.15.5.2

Answer 12.7

Answer **A** — This offence applies to persons in lawful custody, anywhere. It is not restricted to custody units, prison, etc. Answer C is therefore incorrect. Whether a person is 'in custody' or not is a question of fact and the word 'custody' is to be given its ordinary meaning (*E v DPP* [2002] Crime LR 737). This could be shown by providing evidence that the person's liberty was restricted (as it is in the question), and that it was lawful (Sch. 4 to the 2002 Act provides this). This custody is not restricted to sworn police officers and would include police community support officers (PCSOs), Investigating Officers or Escort Officers (who are given powers by the 2002 Act); answer D is therefore incorrect. The offence of escaping is an indictable offence and is arrestable; therefore, answer B is incorrect.

Crime, para. 1.15.9

Answer 12.8

Answer **D** — Section 51 deals with intimidation of witnesses and jurors:

(1) A person commits an offence if —
   (a) he does an act which intimidates, and is intended to intimidate, another person ('the victim'),
   (b) he does the act knowing or believing that the victim is assisting in the investigation of an offence or is a witness or potential witness or a juror or potential juror in proceedings for an offence, and
   (c) he does it intending thereby to cause the investigation or the course of justice to be obstructed, perverted or interfered with.

It includes potential jurors; therefore answer A is incorrect. This is a crime of specific intent, and it makes no difference what the outcome of the intimidation is, provided the relevant intent is present; answer C is therefore incorrect. The offence can be committed against a person other than the victim, as outlined in s. 51(3):

For the purposes of subsections (1) and (2) it is immaterial that the act is or would be done, or that the threat is made —

(a) otherwise than in the presence of the victim, or

(b) to a person other than the victim.

Answer B is therefore incorrect.

Crime, para. 1.15.5.1

Answer 12.9

Answer **B** — Section 4 of the Criminal Law Act 1967 creates the offence of assisting a person who has committed an arrestable offence:

(1) Where a person has committed an arrestable offence, any other person who knowing or believing him to be guilty of the offence or some other arrestable offence does without lawful authority or reasonable excuse any act, with intent to impede his apprehension or prosecution shall be guilty of an offence.

Constable WESSON certainly has guilty knowledge of the perpetrator of an arrestable offence, but this offence is committed by a positive act with intent to impede arrest; simply keeping quiet about what you know is insufficient to commit this offence: answer A is therefore incorrect. Police officers can commit this offence (at least there is nothing to say they can't!) and it is immaterial that the person is later convicted of the offence; answers C and D are thus incorrect.

Crime, para. 1.15.7

Answer 12.10

Answer **D** — The offence is made out where the person who makes the statement does so in the knowledge that it is untrue. His beliefs and actions in relation to checking the veracity of the statement are of no consequence. What is important is that he knows the statement he make is untrue; answers A, B and C are therefore incorrect.

Crime, para. 1.16.4

Question Checklist

The checklist below is designed to help you keep track of your progress when answering the multiple-choice questions. If you fill this in after one attempt at each question, you will be able to check how many you have got right and which questions you need to revisit a second time.

	First attempt Correct (✓)	Second attempt Correct (✓)
1 State of Mind and Criminal Conduct		
1.1		
1.2		
1.3		
1.4		
1.5		
1.6		
1.7		
1.8		
1.9		
1.10		
1.11		
1.12		
1.13		
1.14		
2 Incomplete Offences and Police Investigations		
2.1		
2.2		
2.3		
2.4		
2.5		
2.6		

	First attempt Correct (✓)	Second attempt Correct (✓)
2.7		
2.8		
2.9		
2.10		
3 General Defences		
3.1		
3.2		
3.3		
3.4		
3.5		
3.6		
3.7		
3.8		
3.9		
3.10		
4 Homicide		
4.1		
4.2		
4.3		
4.4		
4.5		
4.6		

	First attempt Correct (✓)	Second attempt Correct (✓)
4.7		
4.8		

5 Misuse of Drugs

	First attempt Correct (✓)	Second attempt Correct (✓)
5.1		
5.2		
5.3		
5.4		
5.5		
5.6		
5.7		
5.8		
5.9		
5.10		
5.11		
5.12		
5.13		
5.14		
5.15		
5.16		
5.17		

6 Offences Arising out of Pregnancy and Childbirth

	First attempt Correct (✓)	Second attempt Correct (✓)
6.1		
6.2		
6.3		
6.4		
6.5		

7 Offences Against the Person

	First attempt Correct (✓)	Second attempt Correct (✓)
7.1		
7.2		
7.3		
7.4		
7.5		
7.6		
7.7		
7.8		

	First attempt Correct (✓)	Second attempt Correct (✓)
7.9		
7.10		
7.11		
7.12		
7.13		
7.14		

8 Sexual Offences

	First attempt Correct (✓)	Second attempt Correct (✓)
8.1		
8.2		
8.3		
8.4		
8.5		
8.6		
8.7		
8.8		
8.9		
8.10		
8.11		
8.12		
8.13		
8.14		
8.15		
8.16		
8.17		
8.18		
8.19		
8.20		
8.21		
8.22		
8.23		
8.24		
8.25		

9 Child Abduction and Cruelty

	First attempt Correct (✓)	Second attempt Correct (✓)
9.1		
9.2		
9.3		

	First attempt Correct (✓)	Second attempt Correct (✓)
9.4		
9.5		
10 Offences Amounting to Dishonesty, Deception and Fraud		
10.1		
10.2		
10.3		
10.4		
10.5		
10.6		
10.7		
10.8		
10.9		
10.10		
10.11		
10.12		
10.13		
10.14		
10.15		
10.16		
10.17		
10.18		
10.19		
10.20		
10.21		
10.22		

	First attempt Correct (✓)	Second attempt Correct (✓)
10.23		
10.24		
10.25		
10.26		
11 Criminal Damage		
11.1		
11.2		
11.3		
11.4		
11.5		
11.6		
11.7		
11.8		
12 Offences Against the Administration of Justice and Immigration Offences		
12.1		
12.2		
12.3		
12.4		
12.5		
12.6		
12.7		
12.8		
12.9		
12.10